S. Hrg. 112–865

IS POVERTY A DEATH SENTENCE?

HEARING

BEFORE THE

SUBCOMMITTEE ON PRIMARY HEALTH AND AGING

OF THE

COMMITTEE ON HEALTH, EDUCATION, LABOR, AND PENSIONS

UNITED STATES SENATE

ONE HUNDRED TWELFTH CONGRESS

FIRST SESSION

ON

EXAMINING POVERTY

———————

SEPTEMBER 13, 2011

———————

Printed for the use of the Committee on Health, Education, Labor, and Pensions

Available via the World Wide Web: http://www.gpo.gov/fdsys/

U.S. GOVERNMENT PRINTING OFFICE

87–268 PDF   WASHINGTON : 2014

(II)

CONTENTS

STATEMENTS

TUESDAY, SEPTEMBER 13, 2011

Page

COMMITTEE MEMBERS

WITNESS—PANEL I

WITNESS—PANEL II

IS POVERTY A DEATH SENTENCE?

TUESDAY, SEPTEMBER 13, 2011

U.S. SENATE,
SUBCOMMITTEE ON PRIMARY HEALTH AND AGING,
COMMITTEE ON HEALTH, EDUCATION, LABOR, AND PENSIONS,
Washington, DC.

The subcommittee met, pursuant to notice, at 10:08 a.m. in room SD–430, Dirksen Senate Office Building, Hon. Bernard Sanders, chairman of the subcommittee, presiding.

Present: Senators Sanders, Whitehouse, Merkley, and Paul.

OPENING STATEMENT OF SENATOR SANDERS

Senator SANDERS. Thank you all very much for coming. We expect other Senators to be entering. There they are. OK. Thank you very much for coming for what is going to be, I think, an extremely interesting and important hearing. And I want to thank everybody for being here, especially the witnesses who are taking time from very busy schedules and have come from different parts of the country.

The reason that I called this hearing this morning is that the issue that we are discussing today gets far too little public discussion. It's something I just wanted to bring up and get out before the public.

It is very rarely talked about in the media and it's talked about even less in Congress, yet it is one of the great economic, and more importantly moral issues, moral issues facing our country.

Today, there are nearly 44 million Americans, living below the poverty line, and that is the largest number on record. Since the year 2000, nearly 12 million more Americans have slipped into poverty.

Now, I understand that, generally, from a political point of view, it's not terribly wise to be talking about poverty. Poor people don't vote in many cases. Poor people certainly do not make campaign contributions.

So from a political point of view, we kind of push them aside as not being relevant. But that's not what I think this country is supposed to be about.

According to the latest figures that I have seen from the OECD—and that's the Organization for Economic Cooperation and Development—the United States has both the highest overall poverty rate and the highest childhood poverty rate of any major industrialized country on Earth.

This also comes at a time when the United States has, by far, the most unequal distribution of wealth and income of any major country on Earth, with the top 1 percent earning more income than the bottom 50 percent, top 400 individuals owning more wealth than the bottom 150 million Americans.

According to the latest figures from the OECD, published in April 2011, 21.6 percent of American children live in poverty. This compares to 3.6 percent in Denmark, 5.2 percent in Finland, 5.8 percent in Norway, 6.7 percent in Iceland, etc, etc, etc.

I suppose we can take some comfort in that our childhood poverty rates are not quite as bad as Turkey, 23.5 percent, and Mexico, 25.8 percent.

When we talk about poverty in America, I think a lot of thoughts go through our minds. We think about people who may be living in substandard housing. Maybe they're homeless. We think about people who live with food insecurity, and worry about how they're going to feed their families today or tomorrow.

We think about people who, in States like mine where the weather gets very cold, are worrying right now how they can stay warm in the coming winter. We think about people who cannot afford health insurance or access to medical care.

We think about people who cannot afford an automobile or transportation to get to work or get to a grocery store. We think about senior citizens, who often have to make a choice between buying prescription drugs or the groceries they need.

Today, however, I want to focus on one enormously important point. And that is that poverty in America leads not just to anxiety, it leads not just to unhappiness, or discomfort, or a lack of material goods.

It leads to death. Poverty in America is, in fact, a death sentence. And tens and tens of thousands of our people are experiencing that reality.

Now, let me just toss out some facts. At a time when, as everybody knows, we are seeing major medical breakthroughs in cancer and other terrible diseases for the people who can afford those treatments. The reality is that life expectancy for low-income women has declined over the past 20 years in 313 counties in our country. Women are dying at a younger age than they used to.

In America today, people in the highest income group level, the top 20 percent, live, on average, at least 6½ years longer than those in the lowest income group, 6½ years. If you're poor in America, you will live 6½ years less than if you're wealthy or of the middle class.

In America today, adult men and women who have graduated from college can expect to live at least 5 years longer than people who have not finished high school. In America today, tens of thousands of our fellow citizens die unnecessarily, because they cannot get the medical care they need.

According to Reuters, September 17, 2009,

> "Nearly 45,000 people die in the United States each year, one every 12 minutes, in large part because they lack health insurance and cannot get good care, Harvard medical researchers found, in an analysis released on Thursday."

That's dated September 17, 2009. Forty-five thousand Americans die because they lack health insurance.

In 2009, the infant mortality rate for African-American infants was twice that of white infants.

Now, I recite these facts because I believe that, as bad as the current situation is with regard to poverty, it will likely get worse in the immediate future. As a result of the greed, and recklessness, and illegal behavior of Wall Street, we are now, as all of you know, in the worst recession since the Great Depression of the 1930s. Millions of workers have lost their jobs, and have slipped out of the middle class, and into poverty.

Further, despite the reality that our deficit problem has been caused by the recession, and declining revenue, two unpaid wars, and tax breaks for the very wealthy, there are some in Congress who wish to decimate the existing safety net which provides a modicum of security for the elderly, the sick, the children, and lower-income people.

Despite an increased poverty, there are some people in Congress who would like to cut or end Social Security, Medicare, Medicaid, food stamps, LIHEAP, nutrition programs, and help for the disabled and the elderly.

To the degree that they are successful, there is no question in my mind that many more thousands of Americans will die earlier than they should. In other words, they are being sentenced to death without having committed any crime, other than being poor.

What is especially tragic and reprehensible is that with the kind of childhood poverty rates we are seeing today, unless we turn this vicious circle around, we are dooming a significant part of an entire future generation to unnecessary suffering and premature death.

This is not what America is supposed to be about and we must not allow that to happen.

Senator Paul.

STATEMENT OF SENATOR PAUL

Senator PAUL. Thank you, Senator Sanders, for holding these hearings. I agree with you that poverty is an important issue. I also agree that we need to understand what causes poverty and what causes prosperity, or we won't be able to fix the problem.

Kwashiorkor is a condition in which the abdomen swells because fluid leaks from the vascular space. Kwashiorkor is a phenomenon associated with starvation and lack of protein. We've all seen the sad and horrific pictures of famines in Africa.

Kwashiorkor is no longer present in the United States. Capitalism in our country vanquished starvation along with smallpox and polio. Anyone who wishes to equate poverty with death must go to the third world to do so. Anyone wishing to equate poverty with death must seek out socialism and tyranny.

Those who wish to see death from poverty in our country are blind to the truth. While we all hope to lessen the sting of poverty, we need to put poverty in America into context.

Robert Rector, of the Heritage Foundation, recently put together a profile of the typical poor household in America. The average poor household has a car, air conditioning, two color televisions, cable or satellite TV, a DVD player, and an Xbox. Their home is in good repair and is bigger than the average non-poor European.

The average poor person reports that, in the past year, that they were not hungry. They were able to obtain medical care and had sufficient funds during the past year to meet all essential needs. This is the average poor person in America.

An American citizen can expect to live a decade longer than the world average and nearly twice as long as some African countries. Infectious diseases such as AIDS decimate third-world countries, while American citizens are often immunized from disease or easily treated for these conditions.

While more than 750,000 people around the world die each year from malaria, the United States has zero deaths from malaria. At the turn of the last century, life expectancy in the United States was about 46 years of age. Life expectancy now approaches 80. By all measures, this is a great success. Mortality due to infectious diseases affects 50 percent of children in Africa and is now less than 1 percent in America, an extraordinary success.

One of our witnesses today, Michael Cannon, will explain how, over time, poor Americans became healthier than wealthy Americans of a previous generation. Only in America would we label it as a death sentence for the children of poor families, to have a reasonable expectation of growing up healthier than the adults of wealthy families did in the immediately preceding generation.

To the extent that poverty is a social determinant of health, much of it can be attributed to behavioral factors. Over 30 percent of those living below the poverty line smoke, compared to 19 percent of the rest of the population. Consider that it costs between $1,500 and $2,000 per year to smoke a pack of cigarettes a day. This is nearly 20 percent of an individual's income at the poverty line.

Obesity rates among the poor are higher than the general population. We're not talking about kwashiorkor in our country. We're talking about obesity, an unimaginable problem for those starving in North Korea or Somalia.

An interesting example of culture's influence on health is known as the Hispanic health paradox. According to a National Institute of Health study, despite higher poverty rates, less education, and worse access to healthcare, health outcomes among many Hispanics living in the United States today are equal to or better than those of non-Hispanic whites.

Researchers do not argue that the Hispanic health paradox has anything to do with genetics. In fact, most researchers believe the differences in smoking habits and a strong family support structure explain much of the so-called Hispanic health paradox.

This context, while important, does not negate the fact that there are truly needy Americans. We all want to halt poverty. We all want to help those in need. I am suggesting today, though, that with a national debt of $14.3 trillion, we must be more precise in how we talk about poverty in America and whom we should target with scarce Federal resources.

We need to ask, are we targeting Federal programs to those most in need? Are Federal programs accomplishing their goals? Are we doing what's needed and are we doing it appropriately? Are some programs creating unnecessary and unhealthy dependence on government?

We have limited resources. We have to ask these questions. We also need to understand that poverty is not a state of permanence. When you look at people in the bottom fifth of the economic ladder, those at the bottom, only 5 percent are there after 16 years. People move up. People do. The American dream does exist.

In a University of Michigan study of 50,000 families, 75 percent of those in the bottom fifth make their way up to the top 20 to top 40 percent on the socioeconomic ladder. The rich are getting richer, but the poor are getting richer even faster. U.S. Treasury statistics showed that 86 percent of those in the bottom 20 percent of the economic ladder move to a higher level.

We need to be proud of the American dream and promote policies that encourage the economic growth that allows so many to rise up out of poverty.

In the half of the century since LBJ's war on poverty began, we have spent $16 trillion to fight poverty. We now spend over $900 billion a year and have over 70 means-tested welfare programs under 13 government agencies, yet thanks or no thanks to the Federal Government, we now have more poverty, as measured by the government, than we did in the 1970s.

An all-time high, 40 million Americans depend on food stamps and 64 million are enrolled in Medicaid. If poverty is a death sentence, it is a big government that has acted as the judge and jury, conscripting poor Americans to a lifetime of dependency on a broken and ineffective Federal Government.

One of the fastest growing poverty programs is food stamps. The cost of the food stamp program has doubled just since 2007. There is evidence that the program actually leads to higher rates of obesity. An Ohio State University researcher has calculated that, controlling for socioeconomic status, all things being equal, women who receive food stamps were more likely to be overweight than nonrecipients.

When we've tried to place restrictions and say, "you can't buy junk food," Federal Government has said, "no, we can't place restrictions on food stamps." A recent article pointed out that 30 percent of the inmates in Polk County, IA were receiving food stamps illegally. In Wisconsin, fraud is so rampant, prosecutors have given up going after the common cause of abuse, such as selling food stamp cards online.

There's so much of it they can't even keep up with it. Leroy Fick won $2 million—I'm pretty close to finishing up; I have just another minute or 2, please—won $2 million in the lottery, and yet he still gets food stamps because there is no limit to food stamps based on assets.

In America, capitalism has been so successful in alleviating poverty, that our doctors travel around the world. Doctors today that are here, such as Dr. Tim Hulsey, not only help indigent patients in this country, but travel to, many times, Guatemala to repair children with cleft palate.

As a physician, both Dr. Hulsey and I have treated children from Central America. We have treated children from around the world. Not only are we doing such a good job treating poverty in our country, we're able to send our efforts around the world to help thousands of cataract patients, thousands of those with cleft palate.

So what I would say here today is that not only is poverty not a death sentence in our country, capitalism has done such wonderful things to lift people out of poverty, that we are now helping the world, that really, there are still true pockets of poverty around the world.

So I think, rather than bemoan or belabor something that really, truly is something that is overwhelmingly being treated in our country, we should maybe give more credit to the American system, the American dream, and give credit to what capitalism has done to draw us up out of poverty in this country. Thank you very much.

Senator SANDERS. Thank you very much. We have a wonderful and distinguished panel. Let me introduce our first witness, and that is Dr. Sarah Kemble, who is a practicing physician and founder of the Community Health Center of Franklin County in Turners Falls in Northfield, MA.

In addition to providing direct care to the medically underserved population of Franklin County, Dr. Kemble is a hospitalist and vice-president of the medical staff at Bay State Franklin Medical Center and past chair of the department of medicine.

Dr. Kemble, thanks very much for being with us. And why don't you take about 6 minutes each, if you could, please?

STATEMENT OF SARAH KEMBLE, M.D., MPH, PRACTITIONER AND FOUNDER, COMMUNITY HEALTH CENTER OF FRANKLIN COUNTY, TURNERS FALLS, MA

Dr. KEMBLE. Thank you. I very much appreciate this opportunity to address the question, is poverty a death sentence? Since time is short, today, I'll just share a few clinical stories from my experience in Franklin County, MA, where I founded a rural community health center in 1995.

One of our first board members was a woman in her 50s who was very committed to our health center. She was also our patient, having spent more than a decade uninsured and without access to routine medical care.

On her first routine exam, there was a large irregular abdominal mass. She died a year later from colon cancer, a preventable disease that we routinely screen for in primary care. She would not have died if diagnosed earlier.

This patient taught me one important point about access to care for the working poor. She and many of our patients came to us because the health center was open to all. She felt that she was both using, but also contributing, to a community resource, not asking for charity. And she was correct.

Many working people make this distinction and will not seek charity care. Another case was a man in his 50s with aortic stenosis. Aortic stenosis is a common degenerative heart valve disease in which the valve becomes sclerotic and stiff over time. Eventually, it will no longer open, despite the heart's increasing efforts to pump against it.

When this occurs, the patient experiences chest pain followed by sudden loss of consciousness. Usually, death follows within minutes. Medicine alone is useless for this condition and can even be harmful in the late stages. The only treatment for aortic stenosis is surgery to replace the damaged valve.

This patient worked for a local transportation company which did not provide paid sick leave or health insurance. When he first came to our office, he could barely walk and used a cane. The diagnosis was easy to make on the first visit. Within a few weeks, medicines were effective at removing over 40 pounds of fluid from his body.

This gave him significant relief from his fatigue, swelling, and shortness of breath. He was able to get rid of the cane and said he hadn't felt so good in years. I insisted, at each visit, that he needed valve replacement surgery or he would die. He allowed me to refer him to the cardiothoracic surgeon and he learned what the surgery and rehab would entail.

More than once, he considered scheduling the operation, only to postpone it, as he could not figure out how he would be able to afford the out-of-pocket cost or the time off from work. About 2 years after his diagnosis, he died one morning at work.

Today, I understand there is discussion here about shifting even more costs onto patients. You can see, from my perspective, this makes no sense. For anyone lacking resources, the natural consequence of any out-of-pocket cost is that they withhold needed care from themselves with devastating clinical consequences and at high cost to society.

I will end with one more patient. This was a young man in his 40s, admitted to the intensive care unit with a massive heart attack. His cardiogram and blood work indicated the heart attack had started a couple of days earlier. He admitted he'd tried to tough out the chest pain at home, but could no longer do so once he found himself unable to breathe.

The disease had most likely destroyed a large area of his heart muscle. He reminded me that a couple of years earlier, he had seen me once in our office, where I'd advised him to take a low-dose aspirin and prescribed a blood pressure-lowering beta blocker. Both of these are inexpensive medications with good evidence that they protect patients from stroke and heart attack.

He was a truck driver with no benefits or health insurance and he could neither afford his medicines, nor take time off to follow up with his care. Paradoxically, without routine medical care and a couple of generic medications that might have prevented his heart attack, this patient would most likely become disabled, never again able to resume his occupation.

In concluding, these are just three patient stories, but there are many, many more. Any rural primary care doctor could tell you hundreds of their own and I think our urban colleagues might have a slightly different twist, but the moral of the story is the same.

Our healthcare system can do much better for our people of this country. I wish you all the best in your efforts to enact better healthcare and social policies for us all, and I thank you for this opportunity to provide my perspective today. I look forward to your questions.

[The prepared statement of Dr. Kemble follows:]

PREPARED STATEMENT OF SARAH KEMBLE, M.D., MPH

The title of my presentation today is borrowed from medical slang, "Found down" is a frequently documented reason why patients, particularly the elderly, are brought to hospital emergency departments. I will say more about this later, but want to begin and end by saying that our health care system, in particular our primary care, should also be "found down" by you today.

I appreciate the opportunity to come before you in order to address the urgent question: "Is poverty a death sentence?" As a rural general internist I can tell you that in my experience of the last 15 years, in many instances, it is.

The World Health Organization* has shown in a recent extensive study that the underlying health of any population is primarily due to social determinants. Health status is generally predictable for individuals based on their level of education, income, occupation, geography and gender. Poverty is one of the most powerful predictors of poor health status and outcomes. Dr. Braveman's presentation today describes some of the biological mechanisms for this. I will share my clinical observations from my experience spent caring for poor and underserved populations in Franklin County, MA, where I founded a community health center in 1995.

While the poor literally start life with the cards stacked against their health and longevity, my life's work of creating access to care has convinced me that having access to medical care can mitigate, and lacking access can aggravate these predetermined disparities.

Our health center was started with a planning grant from the State Medicaid agency. At that time there were large numbers of patients in our community who were enrolled Medicaid recipients but they nonetheless had no access to actual care, because there were almost no local physicians accepting Medicaid insurance. This showed me early on that access to insurance and access to care were not the same thing.

Six months after opening the practice, we found that 75% of our patients were uninsured. Many were extremely sick. I remember a woman who came in complaining of rib pain. I only saw her once, as she died almost immediately of widespread lung cancer after receiving the diagnosis from a simple chest x-ray that she had not previously been able to afford.

Another woman was brought in by her family over her increasingly feeble objections after she became nearly comatose. She had end stage liver disease and also died within weeks.

One of our first board members was a woman in her 50s who was very committed to the health center. She was also our patient, after years being uninsured and having no medical care. On her first routine exam in years there was a large, irregular abdominal mass. She died about a year later from colorectal cancer—a condition that we routinely screen for in primary care, and should detect in time to treat effectively in almost all cases.

An elderly man came to the health center with extremely disfiguring basal cell carcinoma of the face that had been present for over 20 years. Basal cell carcinoma is the most curable cancer of the skin, and the slowest growing. It never spreads through the blood, only locally and only after decades when left untreated does it become capable of destroying adjacent tissue. This patient, a logger who lived in the woods, had come of age during the depression and never accepted anything for which he could not pay. When I met him his entire nose and left eye were destroyed by tumor, and he wore a patch over the left side of his face to conceal his gruesome appearance. He died soon after of overwhelming infection and encephalitis after the tumor finally spread through his eye socket, opening up a direct pathway for infection to reach his brain.

This case illustrates an important point about access to care for the working poor. This patient only came to see me because the community health center was open to all regardless of income or ability to pay. The patient felt he was using a community resource, not asking for charity, and he was correct. Many people make this distinction.

Most community health centers provide primary medical, dental, behavioral and pharmacy services, and we take the simple approach that dignified, high quality health care is a right in any wealthy and civilized society. Many of our patients sought help from us with this understanding, even after going for years or even decades without seeking care before our health center came into existence.

Other community health center workers have had the same experience. Even so, for the patients who come to us with advanced cancers or surgical diseases, we can only bear helpless witness as, in many cases, they die.

A relatively young woman who was unable to afford routine gynecologic care for nearly 20 years died of a huge tumor which was technically not even malignant, but had grown so large it had already destroyed numerous gastrointestinal and pelvic organs before she came to our office. This was not a subtle problem, and the patient

*World Health Organization Final Report on the Social Determinants of Health, Geneva, Switzerland, 2008.

knew that she had it for years. She obviously could have gone to an emergency room at any time. But she was so worried about financial catastrophe for her family, she kept this problem a secret until it was too late.

There is literally an odor of death that we learn to recognize in our work. The odor hit me when I first walked into the exam room with this young woman, before I even said hello. Since health centers do not usually employ surgeons or oncologists, my job was to refer her to those specialists, where her worst nightmare—not death, but financial ruin for her family—came true.

Two other patients illustrate the same point. Both had aortic stenosis, a common degenerative heart valve disease in which the valve becomes stiff and finally, will not open despite the heart's increasing efforts to pump against it. When this happens, the patient experiences chest pain, sudden loss of consciousness, and usually death follows immediately. Medicine alone is useless for this condition, and can even be harmful. The only treatment for aortic stenosis is valve replacement surgery, which in most cases restores people to a level of functioning that they have not felt in months or years. The recovery time for this surgery takes months, and in most cases patients require close followup and lifelong blood thinner medicine with frequent blood tests.

One of my patients with aortic stenosis was a man in his late 50s. He worked for a local transportation company which did not provide paid sick leave or health insurance. When he first came to my office, he could barely walk, and used a cane. The diagnosis was easy to make on the first visit. Within a few weeks, medications were effective at removing over 40 pounds of fluid, thereby giving him significant relief from his fatigue, swelling and shortness of breath. He was able to get rid of the cane, and said he had not felt so good in years. He wanted to believe he was "fixed" but I insisted at every visit that he absolutely required surgery or he would die. He did let me refer him to the cardiothoracic surgeon and he learned what the surgery would entail. Once or twice he considered scheduling the valve replacement, only to postpone it as he could not figure out how he would be able to afford either the direct monetary cost or the time off from work. He died suddenly at work one day, waiting for the right time, about 2 years after receiving his diagnosis.

I remember another patient who also tried to wait with aortic stenosis. She actually made it to the emergency department when she passed out while driving on the day when her valve finally, inevitably no longer worked. She underwent emergency valve replacement surgery and lived to become bankrupted and disabled by depression.

The financial fears that lead so many patients, including this one, to withhold medical care from themselves, are neither irrational nor trivial. Her husband committed suicide by burning their home with himself in it after it was lost to foreclosure.

Since this is the subcommittee on primary care and aging, I would also like to talk a little about older patients, by returning to the title of my presentation. "Found down" is common medical shorthand used to describe a patient, usually elderly, who has been brought to the hospital after having lost consciousness at an unknown time, for an unknown reason, while alone.

This scenario is not rare. When it happens, the first thing we try to figure out is the duration of the "down time," as this is inversely related to the patient's chances of having reasonably functioning kidneys, liver, heart and brain tissue. This in turn generally determines whether survival can be expected. The last case I had was only a couple of weeks ago. The patient never woke up before dying days later in the intensive care unit after withdrawal of the ventilator that it turned out she had not wanted in the first place.

Every day in our country, seniors are found down. The risk factor for ending life in this way is being old, sick and alone. Aging and illness are not necessarily preventable, but in our society, being alone at this time of life is widespread. Who among us could not easily end our days in just this way? Most need to pay for simple personal care out-of-pocket and they simply cannot afford it. Seniors all have medical insurance, but Medicare does not cover low-cost home care which would keep them safely and securely in their homes. This could save their loved ones the anguish of never being able to know what happened, or how much pain and suffering was involved.

Today I understand there is discussion about shifting even more cost onto seniors themselves. This makes no sense. You can see from my perspective that for anyone lacking resources, the natural consequence of any cost shifting or out-of-pocket costs is that they simply withhold needed care from themselves, often with devastating consequences.

Our primary care system itself may soon be found down. In case this happens, here is my prediction for explaining the scenario: we will have to admit that we were not able to maintain our primary care work force due in part to this heart-breaking experience of being forced to watch our patients suffer and even die needlessly, even as we knew and advised what they needed, but they could not afford access to the most inexpensive and basic care.

Home care services, dental care, eye care and behavioral health services are among the other types of highly cost-effective support services that can make the difference for many working people between disability and being able to function as contributing members of society.

Let me end with one more patient. This was a young man in his 40s, whose name was not familiar to me when I admitted him to our intensive care unit with a massive heart attack. His cardiogram and blood work showed that the heart attack had started a couple of days earlier, and he admitted he had tried to tough it out at home until he was not only in pain but also found himself unable to breathe. The disease had likely destroyed a large area of his heart muscle, which meant he was doomed to being a cardiac cripple.

I was listed as his primary care doctor and he seemed to remember me. He said a couple of years earlier I had seen him once in the office and advised him to take a low-dose aspirin and beta blocker (blood pressure pill) each day. Both are inexpensive, generic medicines that have been shown to protect patients at risk from stroke and heart attack. He explained that he was a truck driver with no benefits or health insurance, and he could neither afford his medicines nor take time off from work to follow up with his care. Yet to not being able to afford routine care and a couple of generic medicines that might have prevented this heart attack, he would most likely never again work in his occupation.

In conclusion, although I have altered identifying details to protect my patients' privacy, the medical facts of these stories are all true. There are many, many more just like them. Any rural primary care doctor could tell you hundreds of their own. Urban doctors might have a slightly different version, but the moral of the story is this: our health care system and our society can do much better for the people of this country.

I wish the members of this committee all the best in your efforts to create better health and social policies for us all, and thank you very much for the opportunity to provide my perspective today.

Senator SANDERS. Thank you very much, Dr. Kemble. Our second witness on this panel is Dr. Tim Hulsey, a practicing physician of cosmetic and plastic surgery in Bowling Green, KY. In addition to his work in private practice, he is a member of the medical staff of Hospital Corporation of America, Greenview Hospital, and the Medical Center at Bowling Green.

Dr. Hulsey works with the Commission for Children with Special Needs and Children of the Americas. Dr. Hulsey, thanks for being here.

STATEMENT OF TIM HULSEY, M.D., PRACTITIONER OF COSMETIC AND PLASTIC SURGERY, BOWLING GREEN, KY

Dr. HULSEY. My pleasure. In 1982, after 12 years of post-graduate training at Vanderbilt University, I opened a practice in Bowling Green, KY, a town of about 50,000 with about 300 physicians in a Commonwealth with about 2.2 physicians per 1,000 people.

I have been operating on patients for 37 years and have been in solo practice for almost 30 years, treating some cosmetic surgery patients, but more patients with cancer, burns, trauma, and patients in need of reconstructive surgery.

My policy has been to see Medicare and Medicaid patients, as well as to see those without resources to pay for their care at no charge, when that was appropriate. Since 1984, we have run a cleft, lip, and palate clinic through the Commission for Children with Special Health Care Needs, and this serves a large portion of our Commonwealth.

These clinics are available in most States and are available to anyone, regardless of their ability to pay. There is no excuse for a child in the Commonwealth of Kentucky, or any other State that has these clinics available, to go without care because of lack of monetary resources.

I made a choice, as many physicians do, to use part of my expertise and time to treat those without health insurance coverage. And I am only one of 900,000 physicians in this country who have done the same thing to make sure that services are there for those who can't afford them.

There are 100,000 churches in this country and innumerable civic organizations who have mandates, by faith or by choice, to provide care to those who are in need. These include people with need of medical care problems.

Those people are aggressive and active in their seeking out patients who need their help. St. Jude's Children's Research Hospital is only one of the cancer treatment resources available to all comers.

Emergency rooms in our country are mandated by Federal law to evaluate and stabilize any patient that arrives at their door, with regard to the ability to pay as insignificant.

This certainly is a less-than-efficient manner to provide healthcare. Between doctors, nurses, hospitals, churches, civic organizations, free clinics, and individual citizens willing to dedicate a portion of their time and expertise, there is really no reason in this country for lack of ability to pay to be a death sentence.

Mr. Chairman, I've had the opportunity to see the type of poverty that frequently is a death sentence. I've spent a significant amount of time delivering medical care in Central America.

There, you can find the kind of poverty that, for millions of people, means living in a cardboard house on the side of an unstable, steep ravine with no water, other than local polluted streams, no electricity, no sanitation, where meals are cooked over an open, unvented fire, and where lighting an open cup of gasoline is the only means to have light at night, where children run around, barely clad and unwashed, where clothes can only be washed in nearby streams, which are usually sewage-contaminated.

I have seen adults and children living in multiacre, deep ravines full of trash, picking through the trash to recycle things for a pittance and picking out things to eat. The children run among the feral horses, pigs, dogs, cats, of course, rats, and a few feral human beings. They're exposed to drug addicts and the occasional human body part.

They are surrounded by all manner of infectious diseases and with access only to clinics where there are no medications, supplies, or vaccines. There are incidences of significant infectious diseases among this population, including malaria, typhoid, Dengue fever, and fatal diarrheal diseases.

The incidence of congenital defects is about tenfold what it is in the United States, defects of all categories. And of course, my experience has been mostly with cleft, lip, and palate, and burn scars. This is because of the local environment, lack of prenatal care, poor maternal nutrition, as well as a factor of genetics.

Infant mortality rate there is 28 to 38, depending on the source, whether you trust the UN or the CIA more. And this is four to six times what it is in the United States.

Added to this is the position these poor people now stand in, between armies, and police, and the drug cartels, and there is also a significant poverty of justice, in that 96 percent of crimes in that area go unpunished.

This is certainly the kind of poverty that can be a death sentence. In the United States of America, if people living in poverty cannot avoid health problems by adopting a healthy lifestyle, they can choose, actively, to seek care through the myriad resources I have mentioned, and certainly, some that I have forgotten to mention.

That care is best delivered locally by private individuals and practitioners who can act as the patient's advocate without extraneous pressures. In other words, there is little reason, other than failure to seek care, that poverty should be a death sentence in this country. Thank you, Mr. Chairman.

[The prepared statement of Dr. Hulsey follows:]

PREPARED STATEMENT OF TIM HULSEY, M.D.

My name is Tim Hulsey. I opened my practice in Plastic Surgery in Bowling Green, KY, in 1982, after 12 years of post-graduate training at Vanderbilt University. Bowling Green has a population of about 50,000, with about 300 physicians. The Commonwealth of Kentucky has about 2.2 physicians per 1,000 people, slightly less than the national average of 2.6.

I have been operating on patients for 37 years and have been in solo practice for almost 30 years, treating some cosmetic surgery patients, but more patients with cancer, burns, trauma, and patients in need of reconstructive surgery—both adults and children. My policy has been to see Medicaid and Medicare patients, because many of them need specialized care that would otherwise only be available hundreds of miles away or across State lines. I also see patients who are uninsured and without resources. These patients are referred by other physicians, the free clinic, by a friend or family member, or a charitable organization.

Since 1984, an othodontist, an oral surgeon, a pediatrician, and I have run a Cleft Lip and Palate/Plastic Surgery Clinic through the Kentucky Commission for Children with Special Health Care Needs in Bowling Green. This clinic has been available to anyone regardless of their ability to pay for the services. Such services are available in other States, as well. There is no excuse for a child in the Commonwealth of Kentucky, or any other State where these clinics exist, to go without care because of lack of monetary resources.

I made a choice to use part of my time and expertise to do things for those with no means to bear the expense for it, and I am one of over 900,000 doctors in this country.

Since 1995, Commonwealth Health Corporation, which runs one of our local hospitals, opened the Commonwealth Health Free Clinic to provide Medical and Dental care to the working uninsured. There are about 1,200 free clinics throughout this country. These supplement the community health departments available across all 50 States.

My friend, Dr. Andy Moore, a plastic surgeon in Lexington, KY, runs a program called "Surgery on Sundays" that provides surgical services to those without health insurance coverage. This is only one of thousands of individual efforts by physicians across the country to make sure that medical services are available for those who cannot pay.

There are about 100,000 churches in this country. Most religions mandate a service to those in need, including those in need of medical care. You have no difficulty seeing this in action around our Nation daily.

One source sites civic organizations in the United States as "too many to list." These entities have mandates to provide service to the people in their communities, many related specifically to medical care. Shriner's Hospitals, numbering about 20 in the United States alone, are well-known for providing some of the most expert treatment in the world at no charge. The Lions Club commitment to eye problems is another well-known example. These organizations actively and aggressively seek out patients for their programs.

Hospitals such as St. Jude Children's Research Hospital provide expert cancer treatment to any child regardless of ability to pay for it.

As I said, I am only one physician. Let's be extremely conservative, as I want to be, and say that only half of U.S. physicians are inclined to practice as I do, volunteering services for those unable to cover the cost. That amounts to 450,000 doctors providing non-remunerated care. If you add in all the other entities that I mentioned above, plus others that I have certainly left out, that amounts to a vast resource for anyone in need of medical care in this country, regardless of their financial situation.

Mr. Chairman, I have had an opportunity to see the type of poverty that is frequently a death sentence. I have spent a significant amount of time delivering medical care in Central America. There you can find the kind of poverty that means living in a cardboard house on the side of an unstable ravine, with no electricity, running water, or sanitation where meals are cooked over an open fire, and where lighting an open cup of gasoline is your only means of producing light at night; where the children run around barely clad and frequently unwashed. I have seen children and adults living in multi-acre trash dumps, making a pittance for digging out trash to recycle, living amongst feral horses, pigs, dogs, cats, and, of course, rats; exposed to glue sniffers and the occasional human body part; with access only to medical clinics where there are no medications or supplies. This, Mr. Chairman is the type of poverty that can be and frequently is a death sentence.

In the USA, poor or not, if people cannot avoid medical problems by adopting a healthy lifestyle to prevent disease, they can choose to actively seek care and treatment when they have a health problem, and that medical care is best delivered at the local level, in an individualized format by private practitioners who can act as the patient's advocate without extraneous pressures. In other words, there is little reason, other than failure to seek out treatment, for poverty to be a death sentence in this country.

Senator SANDERS. Thank you very much, Dr. Hulsey. Our final witness on this panel—and we have another panel to follow—is the founder of and physician at the Beersheba Springs Medical Clinic, a comprehensive ambulatory clinic in Beersheba Springs, TN.

Trained as a pediatrician, Dr. Adams retired from full-time faculty at the University of Louisville School of Medicine, where he was chief of pediatric infectious diseases and medical director of communicable diseases at the Louisville Metro Health Department in Louisville, KY.

He currently serves as president of Physicians for National Health Program. Dr. Adams, thanks very much for being with us.

STATEMENT OF GARRETT ADAMS, M.D., MPH, PRACTITIONER AND FOUNDER, BEERSHEBA SPRINGS MEDICAL CENTER, BEERSHEBA SPRINGS, TN

Dr. ADAMS. Thank you, Senator Sanders, Senator Paul, and members of the committee. Senator Sanders, thank you for understanding the great health threats that more and more Americans suffer because of poverty. You do a wonderful service by giving them a voice.

I dedicate this testimony to those for whom poverty is, has been, or will be a death sentence, and also to those for whom illness is a poverty sentence.

These are people I have known, all of whom failed or are failing to get life-saving healthcare because they can't afford it. Most are or were impoverished.

Others were not, but they died waiting for approval by a health insurance company of a life-saving procedure that never came or came too late, such as David Velten, a 32-year-old school bus driver from Louisville, KY, married, two sons. He had liver failure. A transplant was denied by the insurance company, but due to public pressure, the company eventually relented, but it was too late. He died several months after the transplant.

And Cheryl Brawner, 50, a legal secretary from Louisville with acute leukemia—she achieved remission and was awaiting approval from the insurance company for a bone marrow transplant when her leukemia relapsed and she died.

Clay Morgan, an automobile mechanic in Henry County, KY, owned his own business. He got malignant melanoma, was treated, improved, and thought to be cured, but now was bankrupted. Cancer returned. Depressed and unwilling to bring more medical debt on his family, Clay went into the backyard and took his own life.

Velinda Anderson, whom you see in this photograph, I met on Oak Street in Louisville in March. She had surgery to remove blockage in her leg arteries. She was employed, but couldn't afford Plavix, an expensive medicine to keep arteries open. Here, she begs for help for medicine.

Grundy County in Tennessee is the poorest county and ranks the lowest in overall health. Median household income is $25,000. Two-thirds of schoolchildren qualify for free lunch. Nineteen percent of the population is illiterate. The ratio of population to primary care provider is 7,000 to 1, 11 times the national ratio.

On the Cumberland Plateau in Grundy County of Appalachia is the community of Beersheba Springs. My family has vacationed there for six generations. Confronted with seeing my mountain friends suffer without medical care and being forced to pay unfair bills to profiteering hospitals, I established a medical clinic, a free medical clinic.

The following patients are from Grundy County. Charlotte Dykes had an obstruction to the main intestinal artery with stent placement in Chattanooga. We diagnosed a severe blockage of the main artery in her right arm and a 70 percent carotid artery blockage.

The surgeon will not operate unless she pays up front because she still has not paid her bill from the previous surgery. A walking time bomb, she'll be 65 in December when she'll be eligible for Medicare, if she lives that long. In giving permission to tell her story, Charlotte said to me, you speak out for me.

Charlene, 54, hasn't seen a doctor in over 20 years. We diagnosed an acute heart attack in May. She was airlifted to Nashville, treated, and discharged, but didn't fill her discharge prescriptions, including Plavix, and didn't go to cardiac rehab because she couldn't afford either. She's doing poorly now and has a recent dementia, due to small strokes.

Doris, 58, and her husband operated a small local restaurant before her illness forced them to close the restaurant. Estimated annual income, $13,000, no insurance, no medical care. She heard we offered free mammograms. We diagnosed breast cancer.

Paula, 32, cervical cancer surgery 2 years ago, but no follow-up because of no insurance and no money.

Billy Campbell, a 54-year-old tree farmer and carpenter, makes $12,000, has stage-three colon cancer, no health insurance. He needs a PET scan, but the hospital won't do it because he can't pay the $1,500 fee, disability denied three times. This past Friday night, there was a barbecue benefit on the mountain to raise money for Billy's PET scan.

Bob has double hernias. A surgeon agreed to fix them for $500, but Bob can't afford the hospital cost of $8,000. His hernias will not be fixed.

I saw a 64-year-old woman with a crooked arm and a limp. She fell in March, suffering a serious arm and leg fracture. A surgeon agreed to repair her arm in spite of no insurance, but the hospital would not allow use of the operating room because she couldn't pay. Her arm will not be fixed.

And finally, a woman with blood sugar greater than 500 milligrams percent, life-threatening hyperglycemia, five times normal. She knew she had diabetes and she owned a glucometer, but she could not afford the strips to test her blood sugar.

Thank you for this opportunity to speak for those without a voice, who have died or will die as a result of our country's unwillingness to acknowledge that healthcare is a human right and to provide affordable high quality healthcare to every resident.

And this is just a microcosm, a drop in the ocean, of all the people, and much worse in minorities. We need social justice in America, not charity. Thank you.

[The prepared statement of Dr. Adams follows:]

PREPARED STATEMENT OF GARRETT ADAMS, M.D., MPH

Senator Sanders, Senator Paul, members of the committee, I am very grateful to Senator Sanders for his sensitivity to the grave health threats that a large portion of the American population currently suffers because of poverty. He does a wonderful service to these people by giving them a voice to our leaders, so that you can better understand the perilous health care situation so many Americans find themselves in because of their poverty. I dedicate this testimony to all those Americans for whom poverty is, has been, or will be a death sentence. And also to those Americans for whom illness is a poverty sentence.

According to the Institute of Medicine, 45,000 Americans die every year because of lack of health insurance, a stark figure. Surgeon General Julius Richmond, however, reminds us that, "Statistics are people with the tears wiped dry." Today I will tell you about some of those people whom I know or have known, all of whom failed or are failing to get necessary life-saving health care because of financial constraints—most impoverished; others not yet impoverished, but who died waiting for approval by a health insurance company of an expensive life-saving procedure that never came or came too late. The first cases I describe are Kentuckians.

KENTUCKY

David Velten—Louisville. 32 years old. School bus driver. Wife, two young sons. Chronic liver failure. I met David in June 2006. He was initially denied a liver transplant by his insurance company, but due to public pressure, the company relented and allowed it. But it was too late. He died in 2007 several months after the transplant.

Cheryl Brawner—Louisville. 50 years old, Legal secretary, avid bicyclist, friend. Acute leukemia. Advised at Fred Hutchinson Hospital in Seattle to have a bone marrow transplant. Was in remission awaiting approval from the insurance company for the transplant. She waited and waited and waited. Cheryl relapsed and died of her leukemia, while waiting for approval.

Clay Morgan—Henry County. Automobile mechanic, owned his own business. Malignant melanoma. Received treatment, improved, thought to be cured, but now was bankrupted. His cancer returned. Depressed and unwilling to bring more medical debt on his family, Clay went into the back yard and took his own life.

Velinda Anderson, "Help Needed for Medicine" (see attached picture) Oak Street, Louisville, March 2011. She was employed. Velinda had had endarterectomy (removal of artery blockage) in her legs, but could not afford the expensive medicine, Plavix, prescribed to keep her arteries open. She had left her usual neighborhood to beg, so that she would not be seen begging by friends. She had not told her daughter that she was doing it.

Velinda Anderson, "Help Needed for Medicine", Oak Street, Louisville, Kentucky, March, 2011.

GRUNDY COUNTY, TN

Grundy County is the poorest county in Tennessee, 95th out of 95. The median household income is $25,619. Sixty-six per cent of school children qualify for free lunch. Nineteen per cent of the population is illiterate. Correspondingly, it has the lowest county rank in overall health. The ratio of population to primary care provider is 7,122 to 1, compared to the national ratio of 631 to 1.

Beersheba Springs is on the Cumberland Plateau in Grundy County—Appalachia. We have a vacation home there. In the early winter of 2008, Josephine, an 87-year-old friend, stopped by. She was holding her red, swollen face and was bent over in pain. She had an acute sinusitis that required quick, aggressive treatment. I urged her to get to a doctor immediately. She bounced around several places, but eventually got treated. However, her bill was over $2,000, money she didn't have, and she did not have Medicare. I decided to establish a free medical clinic for my mountain friends in Beersheba Springs. The Beersheba Springs Medical Clinic, an all-volunteer, not-for-profit clinic opened in November 2010 (*www.beershebaclinic.org*).

Charlotte Dykes—64 years old. Works odd jobs when able; husband is a carpenter. Peripheral vascular disease. Past history of obstructed mesenteric artery (main artery to intestines) with stent placement in Chattanooga. This spring we diagnosed severe blockage of her right subclavian artery and a 70 percent carotid artery blockage. Surgeon refuses to operate unless she pays up front, because she still has not paid her bill from her previous surgery. Charlotte is a walking time bomb. She will be 65 in December, when she will be eligible for Medicare, if she lives that long. In giving permission for me to tell her story, Charlotte said to me, ''You speak out for me.''

Charlene—54 years old. We saw her in May. She had not seen a doctor in over 20 years. We diagnosed an acute myocardial infarction (heart attack). She was airlifted to Nashville, treated and discharged, but did not fill her discharge prescriptions (including Plavix—see Velinda Anderson) and did not go to cardiac rehab as directed, because she could not afford either. She is doing very poorly and has a recent dementia, probably due to small strokes.

Doris—58 years old. She and her husband operated a small local restaurant before her illness forced them to close the restaurant. Estimated annual income: $12,948. Came to our clinic because of a lump in her breast. She had heard we offered mammograms. We diagnosed breast cancer. Because she had breast cancer, she was able to get TennCare to pay for her mastectomy and treatment, but the coverage is only for the cancer treatment.

Billy Campbell—54 years old. Work: Tree farming and carpentry. Estimated income in 2009: $12,000; 2010: $17,000. No health insurance. Colon cancer, Stage 3. Oncologist recommends PET scan. Hospital refuses to allow it because he cannot pay the $1,500 fee. TennCare denied. Disability denied three times. Barbecue benefit to raise money for Billy's PET scan was last Friday night, Sept. 10, 2011.

Paula—32 years old. Cervical cancer surgery 2 years ago. No followup, because of no insurance and no money. We arranged for specialist care at no charge.

Bob—Double hernias. Surgeon agreed to fix for $500, but hospital charge will be $8,000. He can't afford it. His hernias will not be fixed.

Woman with broken arm—64 years old. No insurance. I saw this woman about 3 weeks ago. She had a crooked left forearm and limped. She had fallen in March, breaking her left arm and her left leg. She went to a hospital emergency room where she was seen by an orthopedic surgeon, who recommended surgery to properly fix her arm. The surgeon agreed to do it in spite of the lack of insurance, but the hospital refused to allow use of the operating room since she couldn't pay.

Woman with blood sugar > 500 mg percent. The normal value is around 100 mg percent. Her's was a life-threatening level of hyperglycemia. We sent her to a hospital emergency room. She knew she had diabetes. She owned a glucometer, but could not afford the strips to test her blood sugar!

Thank you for this opportunity to speak for those without a voice, who have died or will die as a result of our country's unwillingness to acknowledge that health care is a human right and to provide affordable, high quality health care to every resident.

Confidentiality Note. All patients with first and last names have given me permission to tell their story. Charlene, Doris, Paula, and Bob are fictitious names. All Grundy County patients, except for Billy Campbell, were seen in the Beersheba Springs Medical Clinic.

Senator SANDERS. Thank you very much. Thank you very much, Dr. Adams. Senator Sheldon Whitehouse of Rhode Island has joined us. Senator, would you like to make a brief statement for the record?

STATEMENT OF SENATOR WHITEHOUSE

Senator WHITEHOUSE. I'm fine. I'll hold until the questions and we can go on through the hearing, but I appreciate it. This is an important hearing, and I thank you and the Ranking Member for holding it. Thank you.

Senator SANDERS. OK. Let me begin by asking what I think is the $64 question, coming from the testimony of the panelists, and Senator Paul, and myself. We have heard that yes, longevity in America today is better than it was in the past. We have learned that, in the United States of America, healthcare is better than it is in some of the poorest, most desperate countries in the world.

But frankly, I think that gives cold comfort to millions and millions of people. It almost speaks to the rather poor shape that we're in, when we're comparing ourselves to third-world countries, who are much, much poorer than we are.

We have heard from Senator Paul and Dr. Hulsey that, essentially, as I understand it, people can access healthcare if they want it. On the other hand, we have heard from Dr. Kemble and Dr. Adams that, that is not the case. I have quoted a report from Reuters, which discusses a Harvard University study that says 45,000 people in this country die each year because they lack health insurance and cannot get good care.

So the question that we're asking now, is it, in fact, true that people can get all the medical care they need, the prescription drugs that they need, the hospitalization that they need, anytime they really want it? Or in fact, are we having a situation in this country, where millions and millions of people—and let's remember, we have 50 million people who are uninsured—are not able to get to the doctor, or the hospital, or afford it, and in fact, are dying or suffering unnecessarily?

That seems to be the question and we have a strong difference of opinion about that, so let me throw it out to all three panelists. Dr. Kemble, what's your thought?

Dr. KEMBLE. Sure. Well, I think that the nature of our system is that most physicians who have a heart do volunteer and do give some of their time in these voluntary efforts. I think all three of us here have done that. In my experience, actually, before we started the health center, there was a free clinic in our community. And I was a participating physician in that effort.

I also was very curious about what were the real costs and benefits of that model. And I wrote a paper about that in Public Health Reports. It was published 10 years ago. And really, to cut to the bottom line, we did find that the actual cost—these free clinics are not free. Someone pays the administrative costs of running them, for sure, and it's not only that—it's not possible for good-hearted doctors to just show up and do their service without a lot of other organizing efforts taking place in the community.

I was curious about what the actual cost of that was. In our community at that time, it was during the managed care era, so I was comparing the cost of caring for people in the free clinic to what we would normally expect to be paid on a per-member, per-month basis from the managed care companies.

And the cost of the free, so-called free, care actually exceeded routine care through an HMO.

Senator SANDERS. OK. Dr. Hulsey.

Dr. HULSEY. Well, I'm honored to be on a panel with such distinguished folks here who have a big heart and give a lot to patients for no remuneration. I would be willing to bet you that the lady that was in this photograph over here with that sign would have no trouble getting people to stop right there on the street to offer her help for that problem, had she taken that sign to her local health department, had she taken that sign to her local civic organizations, to her local medical society.

I have a feeling that she could also have gotten some response to that situation. There are multiple, generic, cheap drug programs available through many of our retailers. I do think that the resources are available out there.

There is really no reason for a patient not to find a doctor who will take care of their problem with no remuneration, and I think that many of those doctors have the wherewithal to go to their hospitals and find that those entities will also give time for those patients.

I have had that personal experience and, certainly, hospitals are worried about making a living, just like I am. But very frequently, I have gotten patients operated on at no cost to them by going to the hospitals and pleading the case for them.

Now, I'm not saying it's fun to be poor in any country. But in the countries that I've been to outside of the United States, there certainly was no Xbox and the only game being played was, what am I going to have for dinner tonight?

Senator SANDERS. Thank you.

Dr. Adams.

Dr. ADAMS. Velinda Anderson, who is pictured there, Dr. Hulsey, had exhausted her avenues of regress. I did talk to her about that and she was a smart person. She was employed. She had done everything she could think of and had actually made these opportunities.

Generally, it seems that physicians are more open to helping. Physicians are naturally sympathetic, but now, with the for-profit hospitals and with the closing of public hospitals, the hospitals in our area, that we can refer to, are part of chains, large, large, highly profitable chains that sell their stock on the New York Stock Exchange, and they're out for profit, and I haven't had success in twisting their arms to get them to do the surgeries to open their ORs or their PET scan units.

Another point that Dr. Kemble made, I think, is a very important one. And that is dignity. And I have seen the patients in the emergency room and the Children's Hospital in Louisville. And they come in and the clerk says, ''have you got your card?''

Have you got your card? It's a demeaning way to address a person. We need something that provides everyone equal dignity, an egalitarian system in this country, which provides equal healthcare for everyone, just as we see in other developed countries.

I think we tend to want to compare ourselves to other developed countries. I think a comparison with—but in fact, in some respects, we have slipped down into the third-world area, in terms of infant mortality, immunizations, and life expectancy.

Senator SANDERS. OK. Thank you.

Senator Paul.

Senator PAUL. In our town, we have two hospitals. We have a for-profit hospital, HCA, and before we throw all the for-profit hospitals under the bus, HCA has actually been very good at allowing us to do free surgery. I've done free surgery there on children from

Guatemala. So has Dr. Hulsey on numerous occasions, over many years.

We have a doctor who lived in Guatemala, Dr. Schwank, who's a neurosurgeon, who's done many surgeries, also in the hospital. So I think, really, we can't make any blanket statement that for-profit hospitals are unwilling to help people.

We also have a not-for-profit hospital in town that provides a free clinic, as well as free drugs. Actually, one of the main things that they do is, when people come in, they're able to help them with getting free drugs.

Every drug company that I've ever dealt with has an indigent program. I have not come across one that didn't have a program, that you could fill out a card, and send in, and get assistance on your medications.

Everybody over 65 already has assistance. We have Medicaid and has assistance also. When we talk about people—and a lot of the stories were very tragic that you presented—for every story that you presented, every physician in the country can present equally as many so that are real tragedies of people who all had insurance, and still died, and had horrible tragedies.

We have a good friend, of Dr. Hulsey and I, who died from colon cancer. She was an OB-GYN and she had every resource. She had every resource possible, health insurance, physician, PET scans, everything.

And she still died, and it's a horrible tragedy, but the tragedies are sometimes the disease and not necessarily the poverty. My question is for Dr. Hulsey when I ask it. Have you ever seen anybody, any patient, who died in Kentucky, in your 30 years in practice, for lack of healthcare?

Dr. HULSEY. No, sir. I have not.

Senator PAUL. One of the other follow-up questions would be that, when you see sort of patients who are not getting their Plavix and they say it's because of health cost, have you also seen that in patients who have government insurance, who have Medicaid, who then are noncompliant, even though it is paid for?

Dr. HULSEY. Yes, sir. Compliance is a problem in all financial groups of patients.

Senator SANDERS. Thank you.

Senator WHITEHOUSE. Thank you, Chairman. I think, when we've heard the experiences of Dr. Kemble and Dr. Abrams, it may be true that charity helps some people without insurance and it may also be true that illness claims with insurance.

But that doesn't take away from the fundamental problem, that a great number of people who don't have access to health insurance have health consequences in their lives from not having health insurance. In some cases, as Dr. Kemble and Dr. Adams have described, those consequences are fatal.

What's tragic about this is that it's not for lack of funding into the healthcare system that this takes place. The healthcare system burns 18 percent of the gross domestic product of this country. The closest competitor that we have is around 12 percent, which means we're 50 percent more inefficient than the next-most inefficient industrialized Nation in the world at delivering healthcare.

When we look at outcomes around our population, they're no better than some countries that we think of, really, as substantially less modern and industrialized than our own, virtually third-world countries.

So we have this enormous expenditure and we have moderate, at best, results, and that plays out down where the rubber hits the road, where you all live, in the lives of the patients that you described, who simply don't survive an illness because they couldn't access the care.

I hope that that's an issue that we can work on. There should be no Democratic or Republican value in a massively inefficient healthcare system.

My guess is that about 10 cents of every insurance dollar gets spent on trying to deny and delay payment. You probably have seen that, Dr. Kemble, in your clinic. We have a Cranston community health center in Cranston, RI. And when I was last there, they said that half of their personnel were dedicated not to providing healthcare, but to trying to get paid for the healthcare that the other half of the staff provided. I see you nodding your head.

They also have a $200,000-a-year contract to try to keep up with the tricks and traps that are used to delay and deny payment. Then, when they do that, the doctors have to hit back, as your community health center probably did, as the Cranston community health center did, as doctors across this country do, hire experts to do their billing, and to organize all of that.

They can't be as efficient at fighting back at the insurance industry, as the insurance industry is denying and delaying payment. So it's got to be more than 10 cents worth, although I haven't seen good figures on their side.

That would imply that 20 cents of every healthcare dollar is spent fighting over getting paid and not over actually providing healthcare.

Then we have the quality issues of hospital-acquired infections, which cost billions of dollars and should be ''never'' events, but they're not.

There are just a lot of ways in which there's no value in that fight between insurers and providers. There's no healthcare value. There's no healthcare value in a hospital-acquired infection that was avoidable. These are things where I think we ought to be able to work together and try to design a more efficient healthcare system so that the resources that we've already put into the system can get to the people who you see day to day.

I just thank you for your courage and determination, whether through charity work, or through community health centers, or through your volunteer work in trying to reach out to those people who our healthcare system, for all its vast expense, overlooks and abandons. Thank you very much.

Dr. ADAMS. Yes, may I comment on your remark, Senator Whitehouse, about the cost of billing? There's a recent article in Health Affairs to that effect, which compares the cost for physicians in Canada to bill compared to the United States.

And it's four times in the United States, the cost for billing and amounts to some $80 billion. And 20 hours per patient, per week, the average American physician spends doing the billing.

That 10 percent adds onto the 20 percent of the health insurance companies' overhead, so we're wasting 30 cents out of every dollar on the market-based system in this country.

Senator SANDERS. OK. Let me thank all of the panelists for excellent testimony. And now, we hear from the second panel. Thank you very much. I think we have three excellent panelists and I thank all of you for being with us.

We're going to begin with Dr. Paula Braveman, a professor of family and community medicine at the University of California at San Francisco and director of the University Center on Social Disparities in Health.

Dr. Braveman is a member of the Federal Institute of Medicine. She has studied socioeconomic, and racial, and ethnic disparities in maternal and infant health and healthcare for two decades.

Dr. Braveman, a pediatrician and family specialist, has previously worked with the World Health Organization staff to develop and direct a WHO global initiative on equity in health and healthcare. Dr. Braveman, thanks for being with us.

STATEMENT OF PAULA BRAVEMAN, M.D., MPH, PROFESSOR OF FAMILY AND COMMUNITY MEDICINE, UNIVERSITY OF CALIFORNIA SAN FRANCISCO, DIRECTOR, UCSF CENTER ON SOCIAL DISPARITIES IN HEALTH, SAN FRANCISCO, CA

Dr. BRAVEMAN. Thank you very much. Good morning. It's a pleasure to be here. I'm going to discuss the current State of the science that can shed light on the question, is poverty a death sentence.

A link between poverty and health has been observed for centuries, but a body of knowledge has accumulated in the past 15 to 20 years, that I believe makes it very different to consider this issue now than previously.

First, the connection between poverty and lifespan, and between poverty and virtually every health indicator has been established repeatedly. For example, recent studies using national data from the CDC have shown that the poor can expect to live around 7 years less than people with incomes at least four times the poverty, who I will call higher income.

Next slide, please. Poor children are seven times as likely to have ill health as children in higher income families. Poor adults—next slide, please. Poor adults are four times as likely to have ill health and the pattern holds for scores of indicators.

Next slide, please. Because health data in the United States have typically been reported by race or ethnic group and not by income, some people assume that differences in health by income primarily reflect racial or ethnic differences.

But income differences in health are at least as striking when we look separately within each racial or ethnic group. In other words, differences in health according to income are not due to racial or ethnic differences. Most racial or ethnic differences in health disappear or are greatly reduced after considering income.

But is poverty actually the cause? Some economists have ascribed the poverty health link to loss of income due to sickness, and that happens, but by now, a large body of research shows that poverty, because of multiple disadvantages associated with it, indeed causes ill health and shortened life.

Poverty makes people sick. It's true that sickness makes some people poor, but the main direction is from poverty to sickness.

Next slide, please. So how does poverty make people sick? It's not just through medical care. Behaviors are involved, but it is definitely not just through behaviors. I want to give you a few examples.

Your income affects the quality of the housing you can buy or rent, which affects whether your kids are exposed to crowding, lead, asbestos, dust, mites, or mold, all of which have harmful health effects.

A healthy diet costs more. Regular exercise is easier if you can afford to belong to a gym or live where it's safe to exercise outdoors. Low income is stressful. The strain of trying to cope with daily challenges without adequate resources, and I'll return to the topic of stress in a moment.

We have learned that the health damaging effects of poverty reach across generations. Parents' income can shape the next generation's income by determining who can afford to live in neighborhoods with good schools or pay for private schools.

School quality affects children's ultimate educational attainment, which then determines the jobs they can get, which in turn, drives their income. Low income and education are linked in many ways that I haven't mentioned.

Poverty in one generation leads to poverty and ill health in the next, and this is very well-documented. Next slide, please. Many poor neighborhoods lack stores selling healthy food. Children in poor neighborhoods are more likely to be exposed to unhealthy norms and role models for behaviors like smoking and drinking.

Poor neighborhoods are more polluted, they're more violent, they're more stressful. Next slide, please. Recent advances in neuroscience show multiple ways in which chronic stress can affect health and they show that it plays a major role in chronic disease.

For example, stress can cause one part of the brain to send a signal to another part of the brain, which then signals the adrenal glands to produce a hormone called cortisol. Chronically high cortisol levels can lead to inflammation, suppression of the immune system, and premature aging.

Other systems and even chromosomes can be affected. Acute, time-limited stress is not necessarily harmful, but repeated, chronic stress can damage multiple bodily organs and systems, resulting in chronic disease, premature aging, and premature death.

Next slide, please. So who has the most stress? Some stress is inescapable, regardless of income. But higher income means more resources to cope with challenges.

For example, as income rises among pregnant women, the prevalence of major stressors such as divorce or separation, involuntarily job loss, domestic violence, and food insecurity goes down.

One of the most important scientific discoveries recently is that chronic poverty in childhood appears to contribute toward heart disease and other chronic disease among adults, partly through stress.

If we care about chronic disease and premature mortality among adults, we need to do something about chronic poverty in childhood. Finally, the last one, please.

In summary, a critical mass of very compelling scientific evidence shows that poverty, particularly chronic poverty in childhood, is a major cause of disease and premature death overall in the United States and of racial disparities in health in the United States.

Scientific advances help explain how that happens, how poverty damages health through, for example, exposure to unhealthy physical and social environments, denial of educational opportunities, chronic stress, and multiple obstacles to health.

I'd like to close by acknowledging that much is still unknown, but we know enough now about what works to act, to act now. Lack of knowledge isn't the obstacle. The obstacle is political will. Thank you.

[The prepared statement of Dr. Braveman follows:]

PREPARED STATEMENT OF PAULA BRAVEMAN, M.D., MPH

My testimony has two main components:

I. The text (below) that accompanies the attached Powerpoint presentation; and

II. *Broadening the focus*, **a paper published in the American Journal of Preventive Medicine 2011.***

Is poverty a death sentence? What does science tell us? (numbers below refer to the slides in the accompanying Powerpoint file).

1. I'm going to discuss what current scientific knowledge tells us about poverty & health. A large body of knowledge has accumulated in the past 15 to 20 years that makes it very different to consider this issue today than previously.

2. I'm going to show you a series of slides using national data illustrating how poverty and health are related. In each slide, as you look from left to right, income increases. On the far left are the poor—those under the Federal Poverty Line (FPL). On the far right are those with incomes at least 4 times the FPL, who make up around 40 percent of the U.S. population. This slide shows how the number of additional years of life one can expect to live at age 25 increases as income increases. The poor live around 7 years less than the group with incomes at least 4 times the FPL.

---

* The *Broadening the focus* paper referred to may be found at *http://files.meetup.com/1697878/To%20read%20Braveman%20-%20broadening%20focus%20-%20soc%20determ%20-%20AJM.pdf.*

CENTER ON SOCIAL DISPARITIES IN HEALTH
University of California, San Francisco

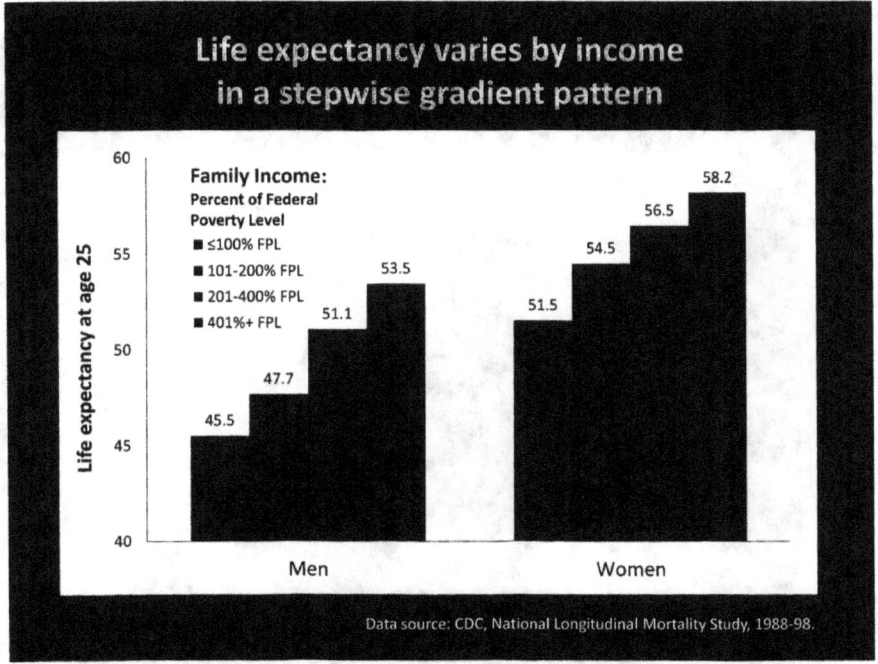

3. This slide shows how ill health among children varies by income. Ill health among children goes down stepwise as income increases. We looked at scores of indicators and all age groups and found this pattern with most health conditions among whites and blacks. In biological science, this pattern—suggesting a ''dose-response'' relationship—adds to a wealth of other evidence indicating that income—or factors tightly associated with it—actually *causes* the ill health and shortened life.

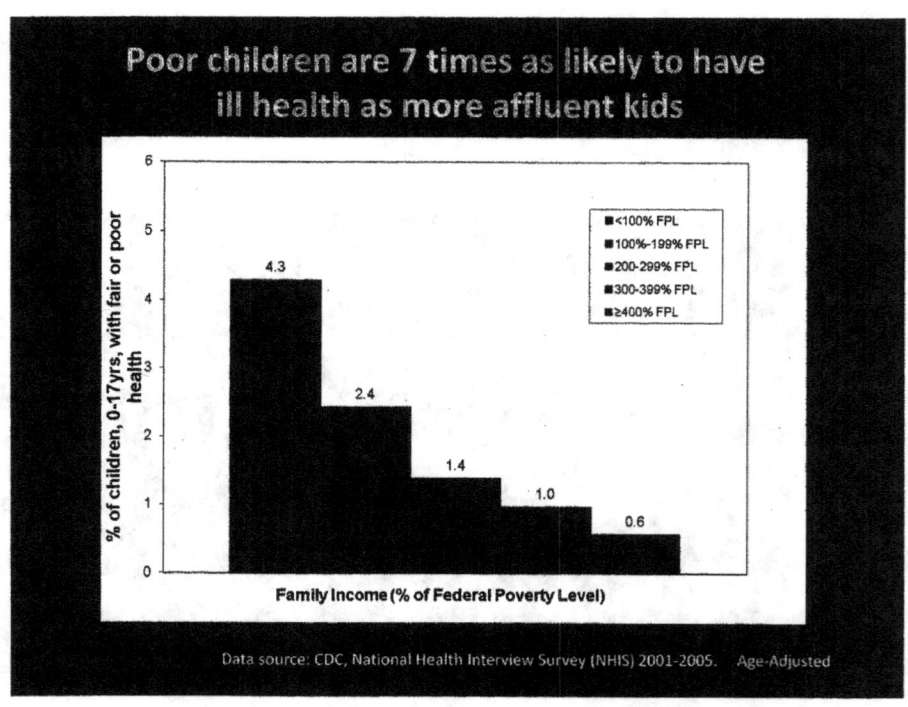

4. Poor adults are more than 4 times as likely to have ill health as affluent adults.

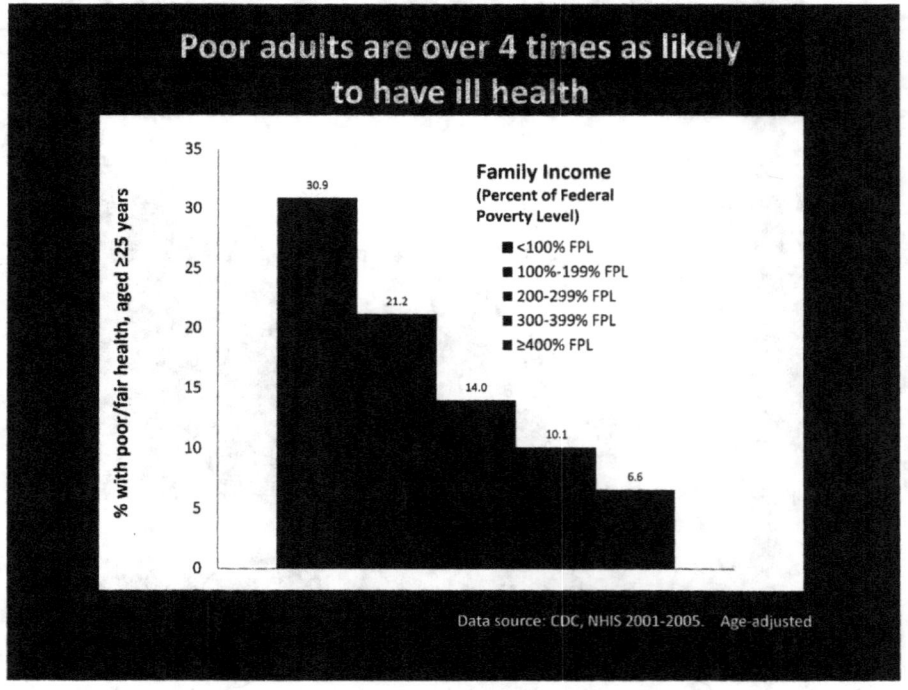

5. Here is the same health measure, but looking separately at different racial/ethnic groups. The stepwise pattern, with dramatically worse health among the poor, is at least as striking WITHIN each racial/ethnic group as when you look overall. This illustrates that the differences in health by income cannot be explained by race or ethnic group. At a given income level, the racial/ethnic differences are modest.

And other research has shown that *most* racial/ethnic differences in health disappear or are greatly reduced after considering income.

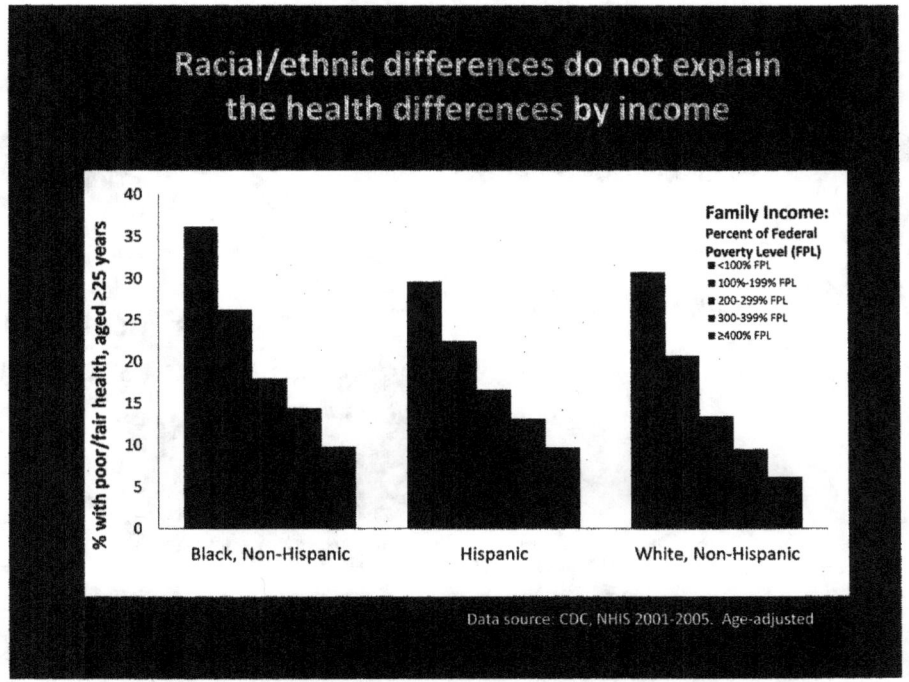

6. What could explain these patterns? Here are some examples of how poverty affects health, for which there is plentiful evidence. Income can influence who gets timely medical care, but that is probably not the largest piece of the puzzle. Your income determines the kind of housing you can buy or rent, which can determine whether your kids are exposed to lead, asbestos, dust, mites and mold, all of which have serious harmful health effects. A healthy diet costs more than an unhealthy diet. Regular physical activity is a lot easier if you can afford to belong to a gym or live in a neighborhood where it's safe to exercise. Many poor neighborhoods are food deserts, without any stores selling fresh, healthy food. And low income is stressful—the challenge of trying to cope with daily challenges without adequate resources. [I'll return to this point.]

How could poverty affect health?

Income can directly shape:
- **Medical care**
- **Housing options**
- **Nutrition & physical activity options**
- **Neighborhood conditions**
- **Stress**

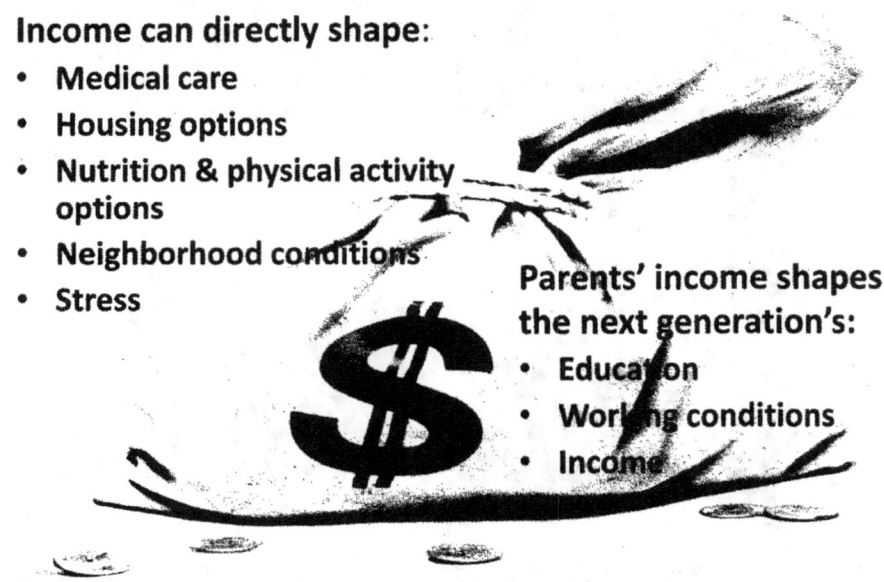

Parents' income shapes the next generation's:
- **Education**
- **Working conditions**
- **Income**

Parents' income can shape the next generation's education & income, by determining who can afford to buy or rent in neighborhoods with good schools, or pay for private schools. School quality affects children's ultimate educational attainment. And education determines the kind of job people can get, which in turn drives income. [And you see the vicious cycle.]

CENTER ON SOCIAL DISPARITIES IN HEALTH
University of California, San Francisco

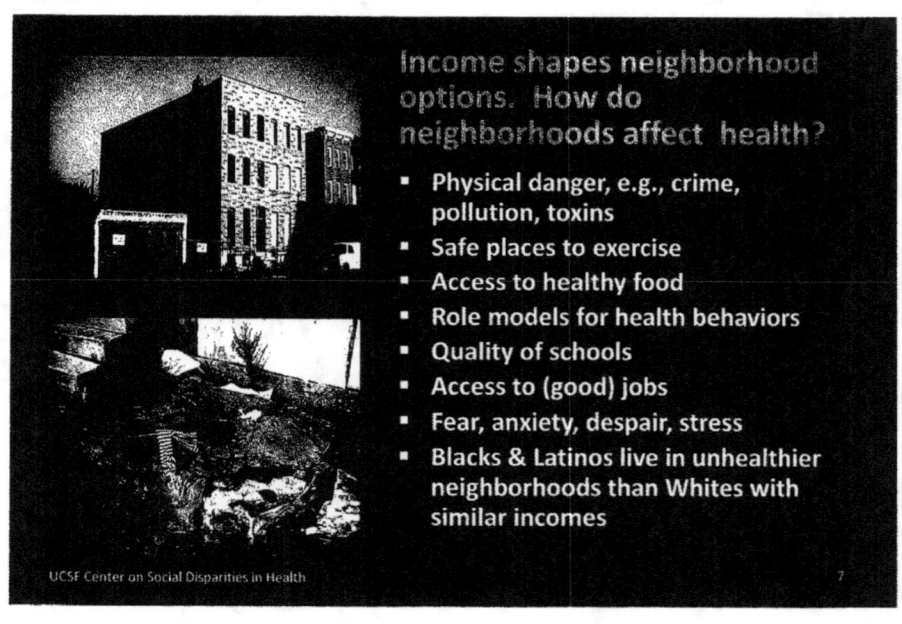

Income shapes neighborhood options. How do neighborhoods affect health?

- Physical danger, e.g., crime, pollution, toxins
- Safe places to exercise
- Access to healthy food
- Role models for health behaviors
- Quality of schools
- Access to (good) jobs
- Fear, anxiety, despair, stress
- Blacks & Latinos live in unhealthier neighborhoods than Whites with similar incomes

UCSF Center on Social Disparities in Health   7

7. I mentioned that our income shapes our options for where to live. Studies show how neighborhood conditions can shape health—this slide lists some of those ways, including stress.

8. I've mentioned stress. How does stress get into our bodies? Recent advances in science show multiple ways in which chronic stress can affect health. This illustrates just one—by causing one part of the brain to send a signal to another part of the brain which then signals our adrenal glands to pump out a hormone called cortisol. Acute stress is not necessarily harmful. But chronic stress is linked with damage to multiple organs and systems in the body, resulting in chronic disease, premature aging, and premature death. Chronic stress in childhood appears to be an important factor in who develops heart disease & other chronic disease in adulthood.

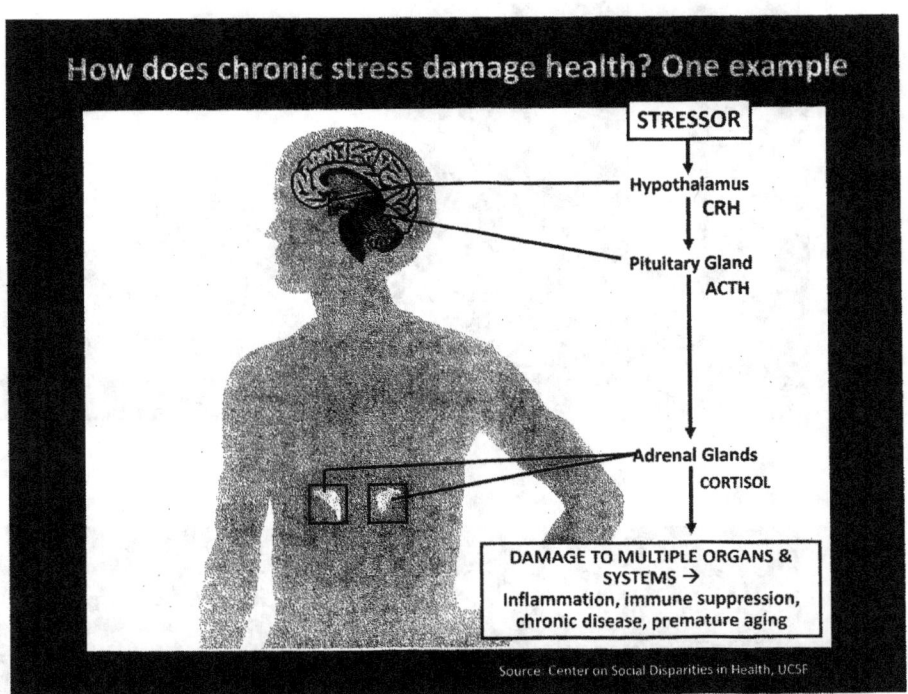

9. Who has the most stress? Some stress is inescapable regardless of income. But higher income means more resources to cope with challenges. This slide shows you what percent of pregnant women in California experienced divorce or separation, according to income. We found a similar pattern looking at 10 other major stressors. Other studies have found the same patterns.

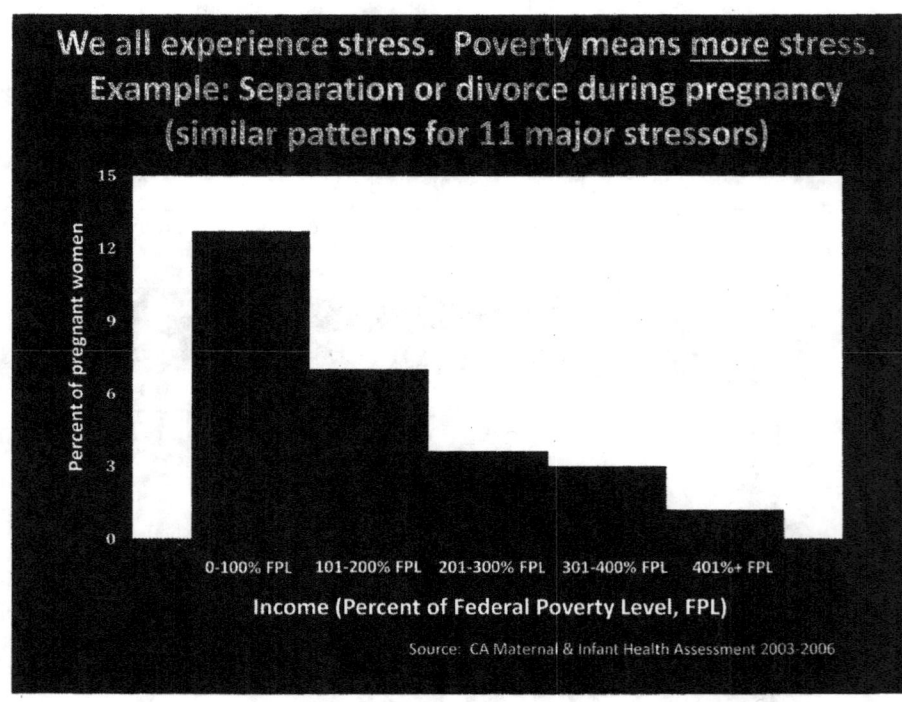

We all experience stress. Poverty means <u>more</u> stress.
Example: Separation or divorce during pregnancy
(similar patterns for 11 major stressors)

Income (Percent of Federal Poverty Level, FPL)

Source: CA Maternal & Infant Health Assessment 2003-2006

CENTER ON SOCIAL DISPARITIES IN HEALTH
University of California, San Francisco

- **Compelling evidence shows that poverty is a major cause of disease and premature death, and of health disparities**
  - Particularly chronic poverty in childhood
- **Recent scientific advances help explain how poverty can damage health, through, e.g.:**
  - Unhealthy physical & social environments
  - Limited educational opportunities
  - Chronic stress
- **Much to learn, but we know enough about what works, to act now.**

10. In summary:

a. Compelling scientific evidence shows that poverty—particularly chronic poverty in childhood—is a major cause of disease and premature death, and of racial disparities in health.

b. Recent advances in science help explain how poverty damages health, through, e.g.:

i. Exposure to hazardous environments;

ii. Parent's income limiting their children's educational attainment which then limits the latter's job options and hence income in adulthood; and
iii. Chronic stress.

And finally, I would like to add, that although there is much we still do not know, we know enough about what works to act now. All we need is the political will. I'm hoping you will create that.

Senator SANDERS. Thank you very much, Dr. Braveman.

Our second witness is Michael Cannon. He is the director of health policy studies at the Cato Institute in Washington, DC. Previously, he served as a domestic policy analyst for the U.S. Senate Republican Policy Committee under Chairman Larry Craig, where he advised the Senate leadership on health education, labor, welfare, and the 2d Amendment. Mr. Cannon, thanks very much for being with us.

STATEMENT OF MICHAEL F. CANNON, DIRECTOR OF HEALTH POLICY STUDIES, THE CATO INSTITUTE, WASHINGTON, DC

Mr. CANNON. Thank you for having me, Mr. Chairman, and Senator Paul. This is an incredibly important issue and I share the Chairman's commitment to reducing poverty in the United States and around the world, in large part, because of the link between poverty and health.

But to identify the problem is not to solve it and there are serious disagreements about how to combat poverty. So I'd like to begin with a little perspective, which is that poverty is actually the natural human condition. It has been the dominant human condition throughout most of human history.

So really, the question for us is not what causes poverty, but what causes prosperity? And on that question, the jury is in, a market economy with the greatest anti-poverty program ever designed, or maybe I should say discovered by humans.

The market economy continuously makes goods and services that the wealthiest individuals could not afford 10, 50, or even 20 years ago, including life-saving goods and services, available to people who, previously, could not afford them, including the poor.

In my written testimony, I show how markets have done so with items like refrigerators, air conditioning, mobile phones, and other goods. The same is also true of education and other crucial services.

The benefits of the market process can be seen in U.S. health statistics. Figure two in my written testimony shows the actual and projected survival rates of men after age 60 from the top and bottom halves of the earnings distributions from two birth cohorts.

Those are men born in 1912 and then born in 1941. One interesting feature of these data is that the gap in survival rates between the top and bottom halves of the earnings distributions is larger for men born in 1941 than for men born in 1912.

But differently, the gap in survival rates between higher and lower income males is growing, but that's not even the most interesting characteristic of these data. Much more interesting is that men born in 1941, who are in the lower half of the earnings distribution, are projected to live longer than men in the top half of the earnings distribution, for men—among those born in 1912.

In other words, the lower income males born in 1941 are living longer than the higher income males born 29 years earlier, and we should all be able to celebrate this progress. Higher income workers are living longer. Lower income workers are living longer. And today's lower income workers are living longer than yesterday's upper income workers.

As a threshold matter, then, governments should not pursue policies and should eliminate existing policies that inhibit economic exchange and wealth creation. Unfortunately, governments the world over adopt policies that reduce economic activity, and thereby perpetuate poverty, often for the benefit of a privileged few.

These such policies include government-imposed barriers to trade, which leave all nations poorer, and trap particularly third-world residents in lives of privation far worse than that known to the U.S. poor.

These policies also include high marginal tax rates. In the United States, excessive marginal tax rates destroy anywhere from 25 cents to $1.65 of economic activity for every dollar of tax revenue the Federal Government collects. Excessive tax rates mean fewer jobs, less opportunity, and fewer goods and services for Americans to consume.

Our first task, then, and our first duty to the poor is not to do anything to interrupt the market process that has pulled billions of people out of poverty and continues to do so every day—to pull people out of poverty every day.

Put differently, our first duty to the poor is not to add to their numbers. Yes, poverty is a death sentence, but only in the sense that life itself is a death sentence. To abuse the metaphor further, if what you want is a stay of execution so that more people can enjoy a long and healthy life, your most effective tool is a free-market economy.

Your task, as stewards of the public fiscal, is not to create a new government anti-poverty program for every perceived need, but to ascertain whether existing programs are wise investments of tax-payer dollars at all.

Now, ideally, that research would capture all of these programs' costs, which go far beyond outlays and include the economic activity destroyed by the taxes that finance them and economic activity destroyed by the incentive such programs create not to climb the economic ladder.

I talk a little bit more about these effects in my written testimony, but a good place to start this process would be to build upon the Oregon Health Insurance Experiment by allowing other States to conduct similar experiments.

This is the first scientifically rigorous study ever conducted of the effects of the Medicaid program, and health insurance broadly, on such outcomes as health and financial security.

I submit that rather than expanding Medicaid eligibility to all Americans under 138 percent of the Federal poverty level, as the recently enacted Patient Protection and Affordable Care Act requires, States could use a lottery to extend Medicaid coverage to a pre-determined number of residents with incomes below that threshold, and then measure the results.

Armed with that information, policymakers could determine whether they would save more lives by expanding Medicare, Medicaid, or by funding smaller programs targeted at vulnerable populations with highly effective treatments, for example, programs offering hypertension screening and treatment to low-income adults.

Such experiments would cost the Treasury far less than the Medicaid expansion mandated by the new healthcare law and could yield further savings while helping to save lives.

I thank you very much for the opportunity to share my thoughts and I look forward to your questions.

[The prepared statement of Mr. Cannon follows:]

PREPARED STATEMENT OF MICHAEL F. CANNON [1]

Thank you, Chairman Sanders and Ranking Member Paul for the opportunity to speak with you today about the relationship between poverty and health, and how government should address these goals.

Any sincere effort to grapple with the problems of poverty must begin with the understanding that poverty has been the natural state of affairs throughout human history. Only in the past few hundred years have humans struck upon the antidote to poverty. Rather than begin our inquiry with the question, "What are the causes of poverty and how can we eradicate them?", we must instead begin by asking, "What are the causes of prosperity and how may we promote them?"

This was the very aim of Adam Smith's volume *An Inquiry into the Nature and Causes of the Wealth of Nations*—known to most as *The Wealth of Nations*—published in 1776. Smith demonstrated that trading with others leads to enormous gains in innovation and productivity, and thereby greater wealth. Figure 1 illustrates how rapidly the United States' market economy has made new and often life-saving products available to people who previously could not afford them.

U.S. households officially classified as "poor" today have access to amenities that not even the wealthiest people in the world could access just 100, 50, or even 20 years ago. Nearly all of the U.S. poor (99.6 percent) have refrigerators, 78 percent have air conditioning, 65 percent have one or more DVD players, 62 percent have clothes washers, 55 percent have cellular phones, 53 percent have clothes dryers, and 17.9 percent have big-screen televisions.[2] To highlight these numbers is not to deny that poverty is a problem. It is to highlight that a market economy is the remedy.

Figure 1

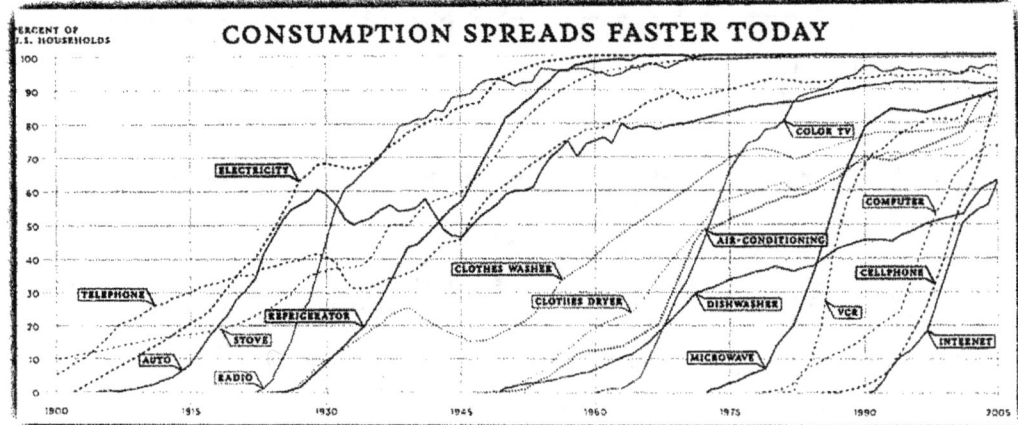

Source: Michael Cox and Richard Alm, "You Are What You Spend," *The New York Times,* February 2008.

The benefits of this market process can be seen in U.S. health statistics. Figure 2 shows the actual and projected survival rates of men after age 60 in both the top and bottom halves of the earnings distribution from two birth cohorts: men born in 1912 and men born in 1941.[3] One interesting feature of Figure 2 is that the "gap" in survival rates between the top and bottom halves of the earnings distribution is larger for men born in 1941 than for men born in 1912. Put differently, the gap in survival rates between higher- and lower-income males is growing. But that is not even the most interesting aspect of Figure 2.

34

Much more interesting is that men born in 1941 who were in the *lower* half of the earnings distribution (the dashed line) are living longer than did men in the *top* half of the earnings distribution among those born in 1912 (the solid line). In other words, the lower-income males born in 1941 are living longer than the higher-income males born 29 years earlier. We should all be able to celebrate this progress: both upper- and lower-income workers are living longer; and today's lower-income workers are living longer than yesterday's upper-income workers.

As a threshold matter, then, governments should not pursue policies (and should eliminate existing policies) that inhibit economic exchange and wealth creation.[4] Unfortunately, governments the world over maintain policies that reduce economic activity and thereby perpetuate poverty, often for the benefit of a privileged few. Such policies include government-imposed barriers to trade, which leave all nations poorer and trap Third World residents in lives of privation far worse than that known to the U.S. poor. These policies also include high marginal tax rates. In the United States, excessive marginal tax rates destroy anywhere from 25 cents to $1.65 of economic activity for every dollar of tax revenue the U.S. government collects.[5] Excessive tax rates mean fewer jobs, less opportunity, and fewer goods and services for Americans to consume.

Figure 2

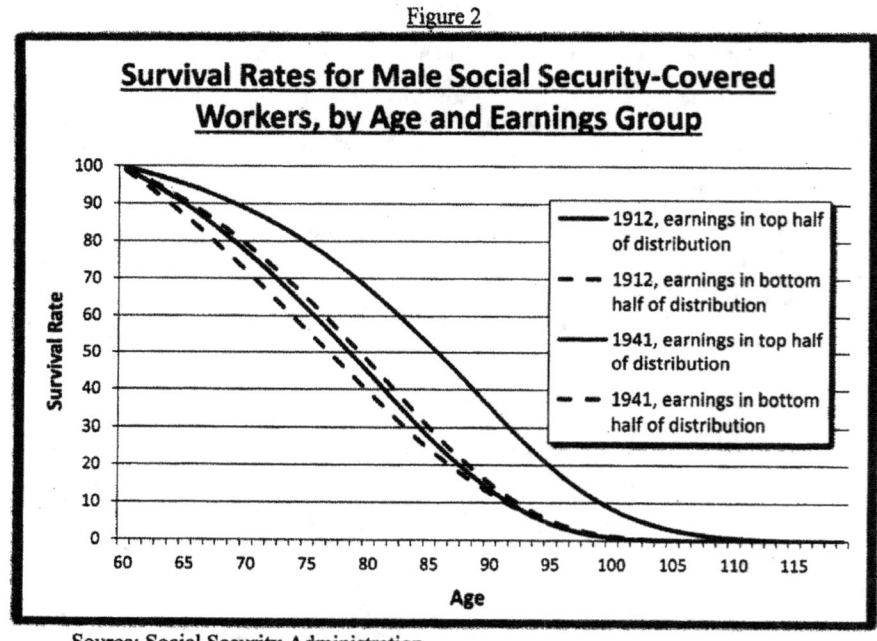

Source: Social Security Administration.

POVERTY AND HEALTH

If we seek to improve lives by improving population health, it is not sufficient to identify a social factor that is associated with health outcomes and throw taxpayer dollars at it. We must first identify the causal relationships between various factors and health outcomes. Second, we must identify policies that yield improvements in those factors and whose benefits exceed the costs.

Figure 3, created by economist David Meltzer, demonstrates the difficulties inherent in the first task. The economic literature shows a correlation between poverty and health, but this relationship is complex. The existence of a correlation between A and B does not tell us whether A causes B, whether B causes A, or whether some third factor causes both. Poverty may cause some people to suffer poor health, while poor health may drive some people into poverty. And indeed many other factors are also correlated with health, including education, social status, health behaviors (e.g., smoking, exercise), genetics, access to medical care, and more. The arrows in Figure 3 show the causal connections between the many factors associated with health. Factors such as income, insurance status, education, and health behaviors not only influence health status but are influenced *by* health status. These factors may also exert an influence on each other.

Figure 3

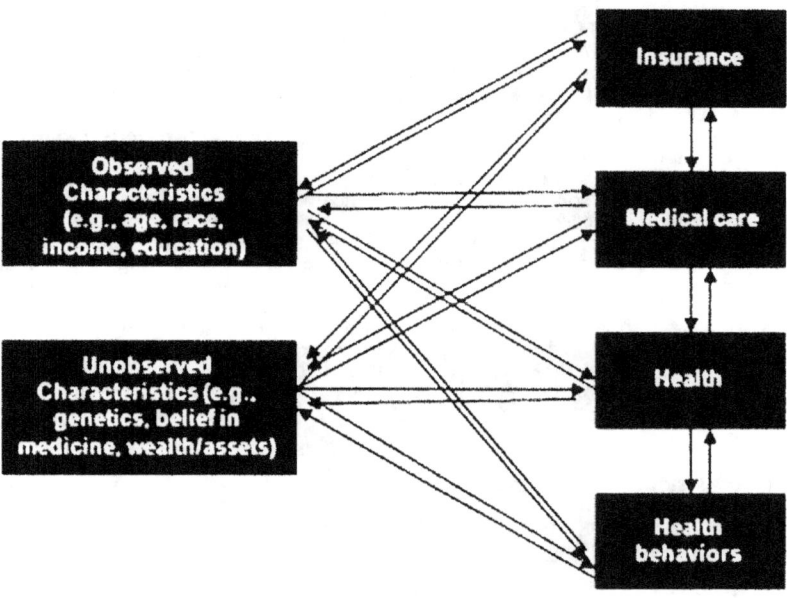

Source: David Meltzer

With so many complex interactions between the factors associated with health, establishing the relative influence of any one factor requires controlling for all the others. In complex phenomena like human health, that means conducting a randomized trial. Such trials are expensive and often impractical. Yet without them, policymakers who attempt to maximize health by focusing on factors with which it is most correlated may neglect other factors that have a greater causal influence on health.

Even if policymakers can overcome this hurdle, it is not sufficient to create new government programs that would deliver improvements in a known determinant of health. Policymakers must also ensure that the benefits of such programs exceed their costs, and that they deliver the greatest improvement in health per dollar spent. Most important, in judging the efficacy of anti-poverty programs, policymakers must look at all of the program's effects, both seen and unseen.[6] Unfortunately, such accounting is usually lacking.

On the benefits side, this means not looking solely at the consumption that the program enabled. We must also subtract the private charity and self-help for which the program substituted. Crowd-out is a persistent phenomenon with government anti-poverty programs. Economist Jonathan Gruber has estimated that, in effect, 6 out of every 10 new enrollees in Medicaid and the State Children's Health Insurance Program would have had health coverage anyway.[7] If the aim of these programs is to expand health insurance coverage, only 4 of those 10 new enrollees count toward that goal. Elsewhere, Gruber has estimated that "church spending fell by 30 percent in response to the New Deal, and that government relief spending can explain virtually all of the decline in charitable church activity observed between 1933 and 1939."[8]

Likewise, the costs of government programs go far beyond the tax dollars required to fund them. The costs also include the economic activity destroyed by those taxes, other behavioral changes the programs produce, and any additional economic distortions.

Programs that offer subsidies to those with low incomes or assets also withhold those subsidies when incomes or assets exceed certain thresholds, for example. The potential loss of subsidies can discourage individuals from climbing the economic ladder. Gruber has estimated that the Medicaid program encourages low-income households to reduce their asset holdings by $1,600 to become eligible for the program.[9] The "Patient Protection and Affordable Care Act" of 2010 (PPACA) offers large subsidies to help low-income households purchase health insurance. But because those subsidies shrink or disappear when household income exceeds certain thresholds, the law creates effective marginal tax rates in excess of 100 percent on low-income households.[10] Those implicit marginal rates are far higher than the marginal tax rates faced by the wealthiest Americans.

The behavioral changes that such programs encourage can have the perverse effect of expanding poverty if they induce Americans not to climb the economic ladder. The fact that the 1996 welfare reforms led to a vast reduction in the number of Americans receiving cash assistance yet was not accompanied by an increase in poverty (which actually fell) suggests that government anti-poverty programs can have very high off-budget costs.

Unfortunately, the political system as an institution does not take the care to identify which social factors promote health, much less target those factors for improvement in a cost-effective way.

The highest-profile example of this is PPACA. President Obama claimed this law will "save lives." Yet the most reliable research to date suggests that the Federal Government's last great expansion of health insurance coverage—Medicare—did not save a single life in at least its first 10 years of operation.[11] Congress rushed PPACA into law without bothering to wait for the results of the one study—the randomized, controlled Oregon Health Insurance Experiment[12]—that might inform policymakers about PPACA's benefits and enable them to ascertain whether they could deliver even greater gains in health and financial security for the same or less money.

CONCLUSION

As stewards of the public fisc, your first task is not to create or expand government anti-poverty programs in response to every perceived need, but to ascertain whether existing programs are wise investments of taxpayer dollars at all. Ideally, that research would capture all of these programs' costs, which go far beyond outlays to include the economic activity destroyed by the taxes that finance them and by the incentives such programs create not to climb the economic ladder.

A good place to start would be to build upon the Oregon Health Insurance Experiment by allowing other States to conduct similar experiments. Rather than expand Medicaid eligibility to all Americans under 138 percent of the Federal poverty level as PPACA requires, States could use a lottery to extend Medicaid coverage to a predetermined number of residents with incomes below that threshold, and measure the results.

Armed with those results, policymakers could determine whether they would save more lives by expanding Medicaid or by funding smaller programs targeting vulnerable populations with highly effective treatments (e.g., programs offering hypertension screening and treatment for low-income adults). Such experiments would cost the Federal treasury less than the Medicaid expansion mandated by PPACA, would reduce future deficits, and could yield further savings while helping to save lives.

REFERENCES

1. The Cato Institute is a nonpartisan, nonprofit, tax-exempt educational foundation organized under Section 501(c)3 of the Internal Revenue Code. The mission of the Cato Institute is to increase the understanding of public policies based on the principles of individual liberty, limited government, free markets, and peace. In order to maintain its independence, the Cato Institute accepts no government funding. Cato receives approximately 82 percent of its funding from individuals, 10 percent from foundations, 1 percent from corporations, and the remainder the sale of publications. Cato's fiscal-year 2009 revenues were over $20 million. Cato has approximately 105 full-time employees, 75 adjunct scholars, and 23 fellows, plus interns.

2. Robert Rector and Rachel Sheffield, "Air Conditioning, Cable TV, and an Xbox: What is Poverty in the United States Today?" Heritage Foundation *Backgrounder* no. 2575, July 19, 2011, *http://www.heritage.org/Research/Reports/2011/07/What-is-Poverty*.

3. Hilary Waldron, "Trends in Mortality Differentials and Life Expectancy for Male Social Security-Covered Workers, by Socioeconomic Status," *Social Security Bulletin*, Vol. 67, No. 3, 2007, *http://www.ssa.gov/policy/docs/ssb/v67n3/v67n3 p1.html*.

4. See generally, Johan Norberg, *In Defense of Global Capitalism* (Washington: Cato Institute, 2003), *http://africanliberty.org/pdf/GLOBAL%20CAPITALISM.pdf.*

5. Christopher J. Conover, "Congress Should Account for the Excess Burden of Taxation," Cato Institute Policy Analysis no. 669, October 13, 2010, *http://www.cato.org/pubs/pas/PA669.pdf.*

6. "There is only one difference between a bad economist and a good one: the bad economist confines himself to the visible effect; the good economist takes into account both the effect that can be seen and those effects that must be *foreseen*." Frédéric Bastiat, *That Which Is Seen, and That Which Is Not Seen*, 1850.

7. Jonathan Gruber and Kosali Simon, "Crowd-out 10 years later: Have recent public insurance expansions crowded out private health insurance?" *Journal of Health Economics* 27 (2008): 201–17; *http://econ-www.mit.edu/files/6422.*

8. Jonathan Gruber and Daniel M. Hungerman, "Faith-Based Charity and Crowd-Out During the Great Depression," *Journal of Public Economics* 91(2007): 1043–69; *http://www.religionomics.com/old/erel/S5-ASREC/REC05/Gruber%20-%20Hun german%20-%20Faith-based%20Charity.pdf.*

9. Jonathan Gruber and Aaron Yelowitz, "Public Health Insurance and Private Savings," *Journal of Political Economy* 107, no. 6, part 1 (December 1999): 1259.

10. Michael F. Cannon, "Obama's Prescription for Low-Wage Workers: High Implicit Taxes, Higher Premiums," Cato Institute Policy Analysis no. 656, January 13, 2010, *http://www.cato.org/pubs/pas/pa656.pdf.*

11. David Jackson, "Obama: 'On the precipice' of health care change, though 'differences' remain," *USA TODAY*, Dec. 15, 2009, *http://content.usatoday.com/communities/theoval/post/2009/12/obama-on-the-precipice-of-health-care-reform-though-differences-remain/1.* Amy Finkelstein and Robin McKnight, "What Did Medicare Do? The Initial Impact of Medicare on Mortality and Out of Pocket Medical Spending," *Journal of Public Economics* 92, July 2008, 1644–68.

12. Michael F. Cannon, "Oregon's Verdict on Medicaid," National Review (Online), July 7, 2011, *http://www.nationalreview.com/articles/271252/oregon-s-verdict-medicaid-michael-f-cannon.*

Senator SANDERS. Thank you. Thank you very much, Mr. Cannon. Our final witness is Phyllis Zolotorow, a Maryland resident and certified medical coding specialist, who has spent the last 26 years caring for her son, whose complex medical conditions have necessitated many surgeries and specialized treatments.

Her husband suffered a serious heart attack 6 years ago and Phyllis herself has chronic health conditions. She will share with us today a glimpse into her life, navigating her medical bills while caring for her disabled husband and son, as she struggles to keep her family financially afloat.

Ms. Zolotorow, thank you very much for being with us.

STATEMENT OF PHYLLIS ZOLOTOROW, ELLICOTT CITY, MD

Ms. ZOLOTOROW. Thank you for inviting me here today. My experience with our healthcare system is as a mother of a 26-year-old son whose serious chronic illnesses started at age 2, my husband's cardiac disability of 6 years, and my own chronic diagnoses.

My husband, Mike, had a serious injury at work, requiring two surgeries and 2 years of physical therapy, paid by workers' comp. After the first year, Mike's employer canceled his health insurance and workers' comp paid for treatment of his injury only.

Mike felt sick in September 2005, but refused to go to the emergency room due to the cost, since he was no longer insured.

Ten days later, he had a massive, near-fatal heart attack with permanent, severe damage to his heart, requiring three surgeries, and is permanently disabled. If a national health insurance plan had been available, Mike would have been diagnosed at the first sign of illness, had a cheaper surgery, and treatment for milder heart disease, and like most heart patients, would have been working several months later, adding to the tax base.

The hospital applied for Medicaid and SSDI for Mike, and Medicaid covered his expenses associated with catastrophic illness and insured his eligibility for placement on the heart transplant list, a life-saving privilege denied any person without health insurance in the United States.

To be eligible for full Medicaid coverage without a spend-down deductible in the State of Maryland, the net income standard for a family of two adults with no dependent children is $392 a month. Mike had to accrue a deductible of $3,500 every 6 months before Medicaid started paying his medical bills for that time period.

Five months after his heart attack, Mike received confirmation of eligibility for SSDI. But as per Federal regulations, there is a 24-month wait for eligibility for Medicare. My spousal eligibility for Medicaid ended when Mike's Medicare coverage began in 2008.

During the 2-year wait for Mike's Medicare approval, I had been forced to choose between applying for jobs without health insurance benefits and losing financial eligibility for Medicaid if hired, most likely resulting in Mike's death or not working and being forced into an unwanted life below the poverty level, thus qualifying him for partial Medicaid benefits and transplant eligibility.

I chose my husband's life over earned income. I have Crohn's disease and diabetes. I was overcome with exhaustion in 2008, unable to get out of bed without feeling faint many days of the week. With the constant stress of being the caretaker for my family and financial worries, I thought I was suffering from depression.

Without health insurance or a job, I felt I could not afford an office visit and assumed I could just think my way out of depression. After a year of suffering, I finally went to the doctor. Being a type II, noninsulin-dependent diabetic, she took a finger-stick glucose level. My supposed depression was actually a glucose level of 500.

I was now a type II, insulin-dependent diabetic and working my way up to a diabetic coma. Contrary to popular belief, most uninsured people don't go to the emergency room for minor illness. Who wants to spend 4 to 8 hours sitting in an emergency room?

We go when we are sick enough to be frightened for our lives. And for those people who think the uninsured are well cared for in any emergency room for any illness, the emergency room will diagnose and stabilize you, but they do not treat chronic illness.

Between Mike's old medical bills and my recent bills, all totaling over $26,000, we get calls from medical collection agencies starting at 8:30 a.m. to 8:30 p.m. 7 days a week.

Since access to healthcare in the United States is dependent upon employment status, I am still uninsured. In 2009, I went back to school. I passed a 6-hour national medical coding certification exam and I still can't get a job. I'm not lazy. I spend hours each day in front of the computer, filling out applications and sending resumes the 21st century way to search for jobs.

Healthcare and employment are so tightly intertwined, they cannot be separated. Getting people employed, and consequently healthy, is what your constituents want from you now. We also want you to defend and protect the new health law that will soon loosen the ties that bind healthcare coverage to employment status. Thank you.

[The prepared statement of Ms. Zolotorow follows:]

PREPARED STATEMENT OF PHYLLIS ZOLOTOROW

IS POVERTY A DEATH SENTENCE?

I would like to thank Chairman Bernard Sanders, Ranking Member Dr. Rand Paul, and the members of the subcommittee for holding this hearing today.

My husband Mike and I are the parents of a 26-year-old son whose numerous chronic life threatening illnesses started in 1987, at age 2 when he was diagnosed with Common Variable Immunodeficiency, a mild form of the "Boy in the Bubble Syndrome" requiring expensive monthly intravenous infusions for his lifetime. When he was 3 my husband's employer-based health insurance company, changed the physician's diagnosis from Common Variable Immunodeficiency to AIDS, for the sole purpose of rationing Craig's health care by denying future claims. The Maryland State Commissioner of Insurance convinced them to change the diagnosis back to CVID by threatening their ability to do business in the State of Maryland.

Craig had 7 surgeries in 3 years, Nephrogenic Diabetes Insipidus, Anemia, atypical Anorexia, fevers up to 105 degrees 5–15 times a month for years, acute kidney failure four times, Meningitis and many more diagnoses. During his childhood, he was followed by 12 specialists at The Johns Hopkins Children's Center. At age 10, Craig was diagnosed with Hodgkins Lymphoma. He was treated for cancer with my UFCW union health insurance coverage. While getting chemotherapy, it was discovered, during a crisis, that he had an Adrenocorticotrophic (ACTH) Deficiency. During treatment for a serious reaction to his previous round of chemotherapy, an insurance company clerk told Craig's Johns Hopkins Pediatric Oncologist to discharge him from the hospital because the "for-profit" health insurance company did not pay for pediatric oncology inpatient stays without active chemotherapy infusions. We took Craig home but 3 hours later he was readmitted through the emergency room with a fever of 104 and complications that could have killed him. *Because of his diagnoses and our 20 percent co-pay of a $250k medical bill in 1995*, Craig became eligible for SSI with Medicaid co-eligibility, as his secondary insurer. Two years later, at age 12, Craig reached his lifetime maximum on my health insurance, so Medicaid became his primary and only insurer. By 1999, I had to leave my job to take care of Craig and his ever-increasing diagnoses.

My husband, Mike, was seriously injured at work in December 2003, requiring 2 surgeries and 2 years of rehabilitation therapy. A year to the day after his injury, Mike's employer cancelled his health insurance and Worker's Comp Insurance paid for medical treatment of his injury only. In September 2005, Mike felt very sick while taking a walk. I wanted to take him right to the Emergency Room, but because he no longer had health insurance he refused to go due to the cost. Ten days later he had a massive, near fatal heart attack with severe damage to his heart and had a Defibrillator surgically implanted. Six months later when his condition worsened he had emergency quintuple bypass surgery. If a Medicare-like insurance plan had been available, (health insurance not dependent on employment status), Mike would have been diagnosed at the first sign of illness, had a much cheaper surgery and treatment for milder heart disease and would most likely have been working several months later adding to the tax base, instead of being permanently disabled.

The hospital applied for *Medicaid and SSDI* (Social Security Disability Income) for Mike and Medicaid covered his medical expenses associated with catastrophic illness. As soon as he received Medicaid approval Mike was eligible to be placed on the Heart Transplant list (without any insurance, public or private, a human being in the United States is denied the "privilege" of a life saving transplant.) To be eligible for FULL Medicaid coverage without a spend-down (deductible) in the State of Maryland, the net income standard for a family of 2 adults (with no dependent children) is $392.00/mo. Mike's monthly SSDI, our only income, was too high to qualify for full Medicaid without a spend-down. He had to accrue a deductible of paid or unpaid medical expenses of $3,500.00 every 6 months after which Medicaid picked up medical bills for the rest of that 6-month period. By the time that deductible was met, *he ended up with coverage only every other 3 months or so, with uncovered expenses we may never be able to pay off.*

Five months after his heart attack, Mike received confirmation of eligibility for SSDI. But unlike Craig's SSI with co-eligibility for Medicaid, with SSDI, as per Federal regulations, there is a 24-month wait for eligibility for Medicare. Why? Only the most seriously ill are considered for SSDI. We have no choice but to believe that the Federal Government wanted Mike to die so Medicare didn't have to pay his medical expenses. Mike survived and is now submitting bills to Medicare. My spousal eligibility for Medicaid ended when Mike's Medicare coverage began in February, 2008, so I became and continue to be uninsured. From the time of Mike's heart attack, I knew I would be the permanent head of household. I immediately started looking for employment. I checked the biggest online employment Web sites on the Internet including that of Maryland's largest employer, THE STATE OF MARY-LAND, but all the jobs I qualified for were contractual, no benefits. I had been forced to choose between applying for jobs I was qualified for, without health insurance benefits, thereby losing financial eligibility for Mike's Medicaid if hired, most likely resulting in his death, or not working and being forced into an unwanted life below the poverty level, thus qualifying him for partial Medicaid benefits and eligibility for a place on the transplant list. I chose my husband's life over earned income.

I have had Crohn's Disease for most of my life and I was diagnosed with Type II non-insulin dependent Diabetes in 2001. I was overcome with exhaustion in 2008, unable to get out of bed without feeling faint many days of the week. With the constant stress of being the caretaker for my very ill family and financial worries, I thought I was suffering from severe depression. Without health insurance or a job, I felt I could not afford an office visit and assumed I could just think my way out of my depression. After a year of suffering, I finally gave in and went to my doctor. Being diabetic, she took a finger stick Glucose level. My supposed depression was actually a Glucose level of 500. I was working my way up to a diabetic coma. I am now a Type II Insulin Dependent Diabetic. During that office visit in 2009, I found out I was eligible for Maryland's PAC (Primary Adult Care) program. It allows me to see a family doctor only, and pays for my medications.

Contrary to popular belief, most uninsured people don't go to the emergency room for minor illness. Who wants to spend 4–8 hours sitting in an emergency room? We go when we are so sick or in such pain we are frightened into believing that our lives are in jeopardy. And for those people who think the uninsured are well cared for in any emergency room for any illness, the emergency room will diagnose and stabilize you, but they do not treat chronic illness. I have had two hospitalizations in the last 2 years with bills totaling over $12,000. With no insurance and without the ability to pay out-of-pocket and with Mike's 2005–8 deductibles of $15,000+, we get calls from medical collection agencies starting at 8:30 a.m. to 8:30 p.m., 7 days a week.

With pre-existing illnesses, even with the Affordable Care Act's regulation of no pre-existing conditions clause forcing insurance companies not to refuse to insure us and out-of-pocket spending limits of $11,000 per year for a family, private coverage is still financially unaffordable for us. Even after passage of the ACA we find that care is still rationed by for-profit insurance companies that threaten our health. Two weeks ago my husband tried to refill his Lipitor, covered by the Medicare Part D insurer, Anthem—Wellpoint, that they have covered for the last 6 years. Lipitor limits Coronary Artery Disease, the main cause of my husband's heart attack and lessens the possibility of strokes. I called the insurer to find out why coverage was denied. I was told Lipitor was no longer part of their covered formulary and I needed to have the doctor fill out a Formulary Exemption form.

The doctor's office called for, received the fax and filled out the formulary exception form, but there was no return fax number on that form. Mike was now 10 days without his medication. I called the insurer to ask what was going on and was told the doctor was faxed the wrong form. In anger, I told them if my husband had any medical issues due to their mistake, we would be filing a malpractice suit and I was contacting the *Washington Post* as soon as I hung up. I was then told the doctor could *call in a pre-authorization* (new information I was never told about with Mike's past medication formulary exemption changes) and they would approve his Lipitor within 72 hours. The pharmacy called later that day to let us know his prescription was ready for pick-up. Over the last 24 years I have become an expert at fighting for coverage and overturning insurance denials for my family.

In 2009, I went back to school and in August, 2010, I passed a 6-hour national medical coding certification exam. I was employed by an MRI facility from December 2010 through April 2011, but was laid off when my employer lessened their patient case load by dropping patients insured by one insurance company due to reduced insurance reimbursements for MRI's in this region. I have been searching for a job since April and I still can't find employment. I'm not lazy, I have been a full-time but unpaid, medical case manager for Craig for the last 24 years and now for Mike, too. I spend hours each day in front of the computer filling out applications and sending resumes, the 21st century way to search for jobs with very little success. I have heard there are at least 1,000 resumes for every job listed!

We have not always been uninsured. In my lifetime, I have had just about every kind of health insurance available in the United States. As a young single woman, I had an affordable individual private insurance policy, then, my husband's employer-based family insurance, for 7 years during some of my son's worst illnesses (I was a rooming in parent while Craig was a cancer inpatient and worked part-time evenings) I was a UFCW union member so my family had insurance through my union, we've had Medicaid and my husband is now on Medicare/Medicaid. I can't tell you how frustrating access to care is without one single affordable national health insurance option. Our easiest and fullest access to health care has been with government-funded but privately administered (Medicare and Medicaid) healthcare coverage.

We are not a rare occurrence in the United States. Our friends, formerly upper middle class, are small business owners. With the economy of the last several years, their business has fallen considerably. They were forced to drop their individual family coverage due to the cost of $26,000/yr in premiums with 50 percent–60 percent co-insurance, co-pay and deductible out-of-pocket expenses for medical care and are now uninsured. Another friend, a nurse, who had to stop working because of medical disabilities, had an individual single insurance plan and was paying $700/ month for about 50 percent co-insurance, co-pay and deductible out-of-pocket coverage. She was finally sick enough to qualify for SSDI and is now on Medicare. Even with an AARP Medicare Supplemental insurance plan, its a great financial relief for her.

Although my son Craig has the intelligence and capacity to earn an unlimited income, unless he can find a permanent job with benefits, not a contractual job offering no health insurance benefits, he will be limited to a salary of less than $30,000/ yr so as not to jeopardize his much-needed Medicaid coverage. He will never achieve the American Dream of home ownership but then, of course, he will never lose his home to medical bankruptcy, either. Why not let people earn as high a salary as their capabilities allow, paying into the tax base *and* pay a premium, based on their income, into the Medicaid program helping to keep it funded while keeping their lifesaving coverage?

Under the status quo, since access to health care in the United States is dependent upon employment status, jobs and health are so tightly intertwined they cannot be separated. It's cheaper for the United States to make sure all of its citizens have access to affordable, quality health care. A citizen able to access care is healthier. Healthy people work and add to the tax base and seek **less or no social service assistance** from the State or Federal Governments. A healthy working citizen adds to the economic growth of the United States.

CRAIG JUSTIN ZOLOTOROW
(D.O.B. 11/30/1984)

AGE	DIAGNOSES	SURGERIES & HOSPITALIZATIONS
2	Common Variable Immunodeficiency (CVID) (mild form of "Boy in the Bubble" syndrome	Start monthly intravenous Gammaglobulin infusions (for his lifetime)
	Severe reactions to IVIG treatment (Migraines, High Fevers, Vomiting 1-3 days after) Chronic Sinusitis (ages 2 – 8) Constant severe viruses Meningitis	Johns Hopkins Child Ctr-1 wk
8	Grand Mal Seizures (2nd to low Glucose from GI virus Physical stress from undiagnosed ACTH Deficiency)	
9	Continuing Severe Sinusitis Right Inguinal Node - swelling	CTs, MRIs, Sinus Surgeries x 2
10	Hodgkin's Lymphoma	Excision – rt Inguinal Node Surgical placement of Infusaport for Chemotherapy admin
	Adrenocorticotrophic Deficiency (ACTH) Hypothyroid Atypical Anorexia Bipolar Disorder/ Asperger's Syndrome Anemia (2nd to CVID) Anxiety Disorder	Dx'd during Crisis in Chemo All nutrition intake thru IV tube Kennedy Krieger Inst inpt (TPN) July-Aug,'95 Gastric Tube (PEG) surgically placed Surgical Removal of Infusaport
12	Severe Gastrointestinal symptoms (2nd to CVID) Growth Hormone deficiency	Colonoscopies, Gastroscopies (ages 12-18 years) Hormone Injections
13	Failure to Thrive	Kennedy Krieger Inst 2wks inpt
14	Hypertension	
16	Fevers of unknown origin (101.0° – 105.0° ages 16-21 yrs) Transient Bacteremia Invasive Candidiasis Anemia Acute Renal Failure (2nd to Lithium toxicity) Nephrogenic Diabetes Insipidus (2nd to Lithium toxicity) Fevers of unknown origin (101.0° - 105.0°)	Johns Hopkins Child Ctr PICU & medical floor - 2 wks
18	Gastritis (Gastric Burn, Bile Reflux from intestines and stomach) Orthopedic issues	Gastroscopy w/ deep tissue biopsies
	Fevers (101.0° - 105.0° - 2nd to Depakote toxicity)	
21	Myocardial Infarction (2nd to administration of incorrect Medication [quadruple IV dose of other patient's med. Levophed] in Hosp. ICU) C. Difficile infection (During same hospitalization) s/p Hepatitis B (probable exposure during this hospitalization)	
22	Neurologic damage & Hearing loss – (2nd to above)	
25	GI Infection; fever 105.4; Acute Renal Failure	
26	Meningitis Acute Renal Failure	1 wk ICU , 1 wk step down unit at HCGH

Senator SANDERS. Thank you very much, Ms. Zolotorow. Let me start off with a question for Dr. Braveman. And I hope Senator Paul will correct me if I'm misstating what I believe his position to be. But we have heard testimony today that, essentially, anybody in Kentucky, I gather, or maybe in America, can get access to a doctor, access to a hospital, access to prescription drugs when they need it, regardless of income. Is that your understanding of reality, Dr. Braveman?

Dr. BRAVEMAN. There is a huge body of evidence that says that that's not true.

Senator SANDERS. Do you want to elaborate on that?

Dr. BRAVEMAN. There, you can look at evidence that comes out of the National Center for Health Statistics, out of the Agency for Healthcare Research and Quality. I know there's the Federal agency's data that are examined on an annual basis. And there's evidence of lack of access to care among certain portions of the population.

I do want to emphasize, though, just in case this point gets lost, that poverty is a death sentence, but it's not——

Senator SANDERS. Right.

Dr. BRAVEMAN [continuing]. Just because of the lack of medical care.

Senator SANDERS. And you made that point extremely well.

Let me ask Mr. Cannon and Ms. Zolotorow. Mr. Cannon, do you believe that it's true that anybody in America, regardless of income, can access doctors, hospitals, prescription drugs?

Mr. CANNON. No. I'm sorry. Sorry, Mr. Chairman. No. I think that cost is a barrier to access to medical care for people who are uninsured. But I think the same thing is also true, or at least my answer is also no when it comes to people who are enrolled in government programs like Medicaid.

There are people in the Medicaid program who cannot access a doctor. There have been deaths of people in the Medicaid program because they cannot access a doctor. I think it's crucial to recognize, when we're wrestling with these questions, that there is no such thing as perfection here. Perfection is not an option.

A healthcare system is going to be maintained by humans, no matter how it's designed, and so we will always have—and former Senate majority leader Tom Daschle makes this point well in his book, Critical—we will always have people falling through the cracks, whether it's a completely free market system or whether it's a completely government-run system.

I think what we have to focus on is, what system does the best job of preventing people from falling through the cracks, filling those cracks in so that we minimize the number of people who fall through the cracks.

Senator SANDERS. Ms. Zolotorow, based on your experience, do you think it's true that anybody in America can access a doctor, a hospital, or get the prescription drugs they need, regardless of income?

Ms. ZOLOTOROW. No. I can't see a specialist for my Crohn's disease. I can't see an endocrinologist. I am extremely lucky to live in the State of Maryland, because I am in the PAC program. It's a program——

Senator SANDERS. Please explain what the PAC program is. Is that a State of Maryland program?

Ms. ZOLOTOROW. Yes. It is.

Senator SANDERS. Yes.

Ms. ZOLOTOROW. If you cannot qualify for Medicaid, it is kind of a partial Medicaid. You can see your family doctor and you can have your prescriptions covered. But you cannot see a specialist to be treated for any other condition. Luckily, there is a free clinic at the Wilmer Eye clinic in Baltimore at Johns Hopkins.

And I am tested once a year for a diabetic retinitis, which Dr. Paul must have expertise in. And without these programs, I would most likely be one of the 45,000 Americans who die each year. I wouldn't be here talking to you.

Senator SANDERS. Dr. Braveman, you make a very important point, and your point is not just that people are dying, or suffering, or losing limbs because they can't get to a doctor when they should. But you're talking about the whole life cycle, of what it means to be poor, the kinds of diet that one has, the kind of stress that one lives under, which contributes to illness.

Can you just compare, for a moment—and I think that's an enormously important point that goes above and beyond access to medical care, which is also enormously important. Can you give us a snapshot? Somebody is upper middle class, earns a good income, has health insurance. Somebody is poor. And maybe especially the impact on the children—what happens? What does it mean that over 21 percent of our kids are living in poverty? What does that mean for the future?

Dr. BRAVEMAN. Let me give you an illustration. So here's a person over here who earns a good living, have kids, kids in childcare. They work. And here's a person over here who also has kids, and works, and does not earn a good living, is poor, is really on the edge.

And for both of them, something happens that makes their childcare arrangements fall through. The person over here has the resources to find an alternative. They keep their job. They are not experiencing the stress of wondering what's happening with their kids.

The person over here is in a situation where there's tremendous stress involved in trying to figure out a way without the resources to come up with a suitable arrangement. They may take chances and leave their kids in situations that are not healthy, situations where the kids don't get the kind of nutrition, or stimulation, or even that aren't safe.

But in addition, the person without the resources is much more likely to lose their job because of this problem with childcare. And situations like that, with a million variations play themselves out, literally, every day and account for a difference in the levels of stress. And as I had mentioned earlier, what we've learned about the way that the physiology of stress is how it gets under the skin.

We know it's not just cortisol. There are cytokines involved. And we know something about telomere length. There's a lot that we don't know, but we now understand the physiology of stress and how it gets under the skin. So that's just one minor example.

Senator SANDERS. I've exceeded my time. I'm going to give Senator Paul an equal amount of time, but let me ask my last question. I began my discussion by pointing out that countries like Denmark, Finland, Norway, Iceland, Slovenia, and Sweden have substantially lower childhood poverty rates, substantially lower. And I might add that they have, also, refrigerators, and air conditioning. I was there. They even have electric lights, you know. They're able to do all those things.

What does it mean for the future of the country—I'm going to let everybody take a shot at this—that 21 percent of our kids are living in poverty, that the number in the midst of this terrible recession might very well rise? What does it mean for the future of our country? Dr. Braveman, and then others, take a shot at that.

Dr. BRAVEMAN. Now, I'll tell you, it's a time bomb. I mean, it's already true that in the United States, we rank at or near the bottom, consistently, year after year, and getting worse. Among industrialized countries, we rank at or near the bottom in life expectancy, as well as in infant mortality.

I think the current science tells us that, most likely, to explain that lower ranking on life expectancy, we need to look at childhood poverty. The growing childhood poverty is going to translate into more and more chronic disease in adulthood and lives cut short.

The business roundtable a few years ago took a very strong position, calling for the need for universal, government-supported, high quality early childhood development programs, sort of high quality early Head Start-type programs, based on the implications for a productive workforce and future medical costs for employers.

Senator SANDERS. Good. Thank you very much.

Mr. Cannon, you want to take a shot at that?

Mr. CANNON. If I may back up to 1996, I think there's a lesson in that year for when we look at childhood poverty and poverty overall. In 1996, Congress eliminated the Federal Entitlement to Cash Assistance under the old AFDC program. They effectively removed lots of people from the cash assistance rolls.

The predictions were, from critics, that this would lead to an increase in poverty, an increase in child poverty. People, a million children dying of starvation, I think, was one of the predictions.

In fact, what happened was, poverty fell for every age and income group, and only this year has the overall poverty rate risen to the level it was back in 1996.

Now, I don't mean to suggest that eliminating that entitlement and cutting back the Federal Government's—this anti-poverty program necessarily caused that reduction in poverty.

But it was followed by a reduction in poverty. It did not cause the increase in poverty that some had predicted, and so I think the lesson from that is that sometimes, government efforts to combat poverty can actually induce people to become dependent on that assistance and can perpetuate poverty.

And I fear, moving forward, now that the poverty rate has climbed in this recession back up to the levels—to pre-1996 levels, I am concerned that, moving forward, and especially in 2014, we are going to trap even more people in poverty and in low-wage jobs, because the recently enacted healthcare law does contain subsidies to help low-income individuals purchase the mandatory health insurance, that this law requires nearly every American to buy.

But those subsidies disappear as income rises. In fact, it creates what economists call low-wage traps that will impose upon low-income households effective marginal tax rates that exceed 100 percent, far beyond the actual tax rates that even the wealthiest Americans pay.

That can discourage low-income families from climbing the economic ladder, so I'm very concerned about the poverty rate in the future.

Senator SANDERS. OK. This is Ms. Zolotorow.

Ms. ZOLOTOROW. I feel that children who are sick, hungry—they just cannot get educated as well as a child who is well-fed and well, medically. And these children are someday going to be the adults that are going to take care of us when we are no longer able to take care of ourselves. And I sure would like to hope that they are all as well-educated, and healthy, and intelligent as they possibly can be.

Senator SANDERS. Thank you. I have exceeded my time. Senator Paul.

Senator PAUL. Yes. The disease of Kwashiorkor, or malnutrition, the swollen babies, the swollen bellies that we see in the third world, you don't see in the United States. You don't see famine in the United States.

Life expectancy has doubled. Around 1900, people lived about 46 years. I remember, in medical school, them talking about menopause being a disease that was not evolved for—or a condition not evolved for because no one lived that long.

It's a hundred years that we have nearly doubled our life expectancy. We should be proud, where we've come. Childhood mortality, infant mortality, infectious disease mortality have all been reduced 200-fold in our country.

These are great successes of capitalism. We need to be proud of our economic system. We need to be proud of who we are as a country. The poor among us are infinitely better off than the middle class in most countries. The poor among us are able to get healthcare at a rate that greatly exceeds the vast majority of the world.

We have had developed nations that have had malnutrition and famine. These developed nations were like the Soviet Union, that plummeted into the depths of famine and malnutrition because of their economic system, because of socialism. Socialism doesn't work.

We have countries like Zimbabwe that have great natural resources and great wealth. And it is squandered because they don't have the rule of law. They don't have a constitution that protects private property. Their leaders run off with their money and the poor have nothing. They have no running water. They have extensive infectious disease, despite having wealth.

So we need to be proud of many of the things we have in our country. And my question for Mr. Cannon is, I really enjoyed when you said, what are the causes of prosperity. It's more important than knowing anything else.

The people on the lowest end of the life expectancy curve, one generation ago, now exceed the ones who are rich at that time. So in one generation, we've allowed the poorest among us to live longer than the rich did a previous generation. That's an amazing statistic and something we should be enormously proud of.

My question for Mr. Cannon is, how important is it, the type of economic system you choose, as far as trying to alleviate poverty in this country?

Mr. CANNON. Thank you, Senator. I think it's incredibly important. The examples you highlighted are on point. To the extent that economic activity in a nation is directed by political systems rather than by markets and market actors, there's a degree of irresponsibility because the political system, the actors in that system are not spending their own resources. They don't spend them as wisely.

And they also are not able to capture all of the information that a market system can capture, through the price system and other mechanisms, to harness the new ideas that people bring to bear on this problem of, how do we make resources more abundant and bring them into the hands of people who cannot afford these resources right now.

So I think that if economic history has taught us anything, it is that a market economy does a much better job of solving the problem of poverty than an economy driven by political systems.

Senator SANDERS. Senator Merkley—Senator Paul, are you finished with your questioning?

Senator PAUL. Yes, thank you.

Senator SANDERS. Senator Merkley has joined us and I would like to ask a few more questions, but Senator Merkley, please.

STATEMENT OF SENATOR MERKLEY

Senator MERKLEY. Thank you very much, Mr. Chair, and thank you all for your testimony. Mr. Cannon, you note in your testimony that Congress rushed the Affordable Care Act into law without waiting for the results of one study, the randomized, controlled Oregon Health Insurance Experiment.

That was a situation in which, essentially, there wasn't enough money to cover everyone who was eligible for Medicaid in Oregon, the Oregon Health Plan. And so a lottery was held, and therefore, gave us one of the first real comparable control—groups type studies.

I wanted to give you a chance to expand a little bit on your observations on that. My understanding is that we only have 1 year's results at this point, and that involves a study of the use of healthcare, the financial strain on the families, and overall health. All is self-reported. In the second year, there's going to be hard data regarding cholesterol, blood sugar, blood pressure, obesity, and so forth, that will be better scientific information.

But what is your sense of the type of insights this might provide to us?

Mr. CANNON. I'll try to keep my answer brief. There is a lot to be said about it. The first part of the answer is that it's very difficult to know the actual impact that extending Medicaid coverage to a population has on that population's health or financial security, because just extending coverage to these people in the control, and then looking at similar individuals, and trying to make comparisons that way may miss important characteristics that are different between those two groups, that might also be accounting for the differences that you're seeing.

So it's important to——

Senator MERKLEY. Such as? Just help us understand it.

Mr. CANNON. If you look at people enrolled in Medicaid and people not enrolled in Medicaid, you might say, ''oh, well, the people enrolled in Medicaid are sicker.'' Therefore, Medicaid must make people sick, or give them worse health outcomes, when really, the reason they enrolled in Medicaid is because they're sick.

You might have health behaviors that's a confounding variable. There are all sorts of confounding variables, so the challenge is to isolate the one variable you're trying to test, which is Medicaid coverage, from all the others, and the way you do that is with what Oregon did, somewhat inadvertently, which is randomization, randomly assigning some people to receive Medicaid.

So you're correct. There's only been 1 year of results so far. It's only self-reported health. There are measures of self-reported health. There was a mortality measure which was not able to discern any difference between the Medicaid group and the nonMedicaid group. The authors of the studies believe it was statistically underpowered. You just didn't have a large enough group or enough years to detect mortality differences yet, but we'll have to see.

There are also financial security measures. Now, I would say, there are improvements in financial security. There are improvements in self-reported health. And you know, people defer about whether those are larger or modest.

I would say that one of the self-reported health measures is a little harder than the others, which is that people enrolled in the Medicaid arm had, I think, 10 restricted activity days per month, due to the mental or physical problems, which is a pretty—you can say that's a subjective health measure. It's a pretty important one and there was some improvement on that score, a half-day improvement.

So the importance of this study is that it, really, for the first time, measures the effect of Medicaid in a scientifically rigorous way. And it's important. That's important to do, not just to establish that there are benefits to expanding Medicaid coverage to new populations, but also so that policymakers can compare the benefits of expanding Medicaid to other interventions that might improve health or financial security, and because I think the only responsible way to approach this is to say, "OK, for a given amount of money, what is it that we're trying to maximize?"

If it's health, then we should be putting that money into whatever gets us the most health per dollar spent. There are a lot of economists who believe that programs like the one I mentioned in my testimony—a discreet program to go into low-income neighborhoods, and screen, and treat people for hypertension—would save a lot more lives for the money than would expanding Medicaid, say, up to all low-income individuals.

My recommendation is that before Congress expand any programs, that Congress do more such testing so that they can really find out what works. Otherwise, we might be wasting an awful lot of money on ineffective strategies to promote what we're trying to promote.

Senator MERKLEY. Thank you. I appreciate your point. I do share the perspective that anytime we can actually collect data on what works and what doesn't makes sense, that we can then utilize our resources in a far more effective manner.

I do think I want to really draw attention to this study because I think, as additional results come out, if it's carefully followed up on, it will provide a lot of valuable insights. The self-reporting was striking. The reduction in financial strain was substantial, folks reported a 40 percent decrease in the probability of having unpaid medical bills, increased access to preventative care. They reported feeling healthier, and putting themselves in good and excellent health, an increase in 25 percent.

It's just kind of a taste of the information that we'll get as we continue to study that process and understand how that applies to providing cost-effective healthcare in America.

Mr. CANNON. If I may respond just briefly, unfortunately, we're only going to get one more year's worth of data out of that Oregon experiment, which is why I recommend doing the same in other States, especially large States.

Senator MERKLEY. OK.

Or continuing to study the Oregon experiment a few more years into the future.

Mr. CANNON. Well, there will only be 2 years of data collection, because I believe Oregon expanded Medicaid to everyone who had previously been excluded.

Senator MERKLEY. Correct. Thanks.

Senator SANDERS. All right. Let me just close. I am sorry that Senator Paul had to leave. But I just wanted to ask one more brief question, and Senator Merkley could participate as well, of course. Senator Paul made a statement—and I think I've got it right here. I always hesitate to quote somebody who's not here. But he said something like, the poor can get healthcare better in the United States than in any other country. Dr. Braveman, is that true?

Dr. BRAVEMAN. That is not true and there's a tremendous amount of data to support that. And you know, what that brings up for me is, you know, we said we rank—I mean, we are No. 1 in child poverty among the industrialized countries.

There's another thing we're No. 1 on, which is spending on medical care. And yet, we consistently rank at or near the bottom on measures of health, like infant mortality and life expectancy. And many experts believe that it's because of child poverty. That's the biggest thing.

It's not about the medical care. It also is a statement about the inefficiency of the medical care that probably can't be made up from within the medical care system, because the inefficiency is based on the poverty.

Senator SANDERS. All right. Let me ask you another question. Senator Paul also made the point, which is obviously correct, as longevity has improved, we live a lot longer than people did 50 years ago, 100 years ago, and so forth, and so on.

But I think the real comparison—and I would say this to Mr. Cannon also—is not necessarily how we compare to people living a while back, with all of the growth, and medical technology, and medicine and so forth, but how we compare to other countries in the year 2011.

Dr. Braveman, how are we comparing, in terms of life expectancy, to other countries around the world? Are we No. 1?

Dr. BRAVEMAN. We have been consistently at or near the bottom among the industrialized countries.

Senator SANDERS. OK.

Dr. BRAVEMAN. I mean, that's where the most valid comparison is. I would also like to comment that I think it's a moral issue, whether you say, I'm going to compare the health of the poor now to the health of the poor 25, 50 years ago, and say, you're doing great, they're doing better, or whether the moral obligation is not to say, I'm going to compare the health of the poor with the health that is possible——

Senator SANDERS. Right.

Dr. BRAVEMAN [continuing]. The health potential that is there. And at a minimum level, that is indicated by the health of socially advantaged people within this country. Even if we say, "OK, we're not going to compare to other countries," because that would be a relatively low standard—to the health of the affluent within our country, on many measures, is worse than the health of lower income people in some other countries.

But certainly, I think one can say that the health of the affluent in this country represents a standard that should be possible for everyone. There is no medical reason why everyone shouldn't attain that and——

Senator SANDERS. OK. Let me ask Mr. Cannon. Mr. Cannon, I've enjoyed your testimony and I certainly agree with you, that when we spend public dollars, we want to make sure that, that money is used as cost effectively as possible. And we certainly don't always do this.

But I don't want to be provocative and put words in your mouth. I wish Senator Paul was here. But I heard—I'm not really quite that familiar with the—all of what's going on in Zimbabwe. I know it's bad news, but I trust you do not believe that those countries that have substantially lower childhood levels of poverty, such as Denmark, Finland, Norway, Iceland, etc, are socialist tyrannies. I trust you don't believe that.

Mr. CANNON. I don't——

Senator SANDERS. Or do you believe that?

Mr. CANNON. I don't know that I would call them tyrannies. But I think socialist is probably a closer description. But let's keep in mind what socialism is, it is the government assuming control of more of the resources that are available in society, and to the extent the government asserts that control takes that control away from individuals.

Senator SANDERS. Correct. But the result is——

Mr. Cannon. And the result is—which results in——

Excuse me.

Mr. CANNON [continuing]. Less freedom——

Senator SANDERS. I'm going to give you——

Mr. CANNON [continuing]. For those individuals.

Senator SANDERS. Do you think it causes less freedom? So do you think, when children in Denmark have a 3.6 percent rate of poverty, compared to 21 percent plus in the United States, our poor kids are freer than those enslaved children in Denmark?

Mr. CANNON. Well, then those enslaved children are—OK. So you mean under the socialist system. Freedom, as I use the term, when in discussions like these—let me back up. There are multiple definitions of freedom.

If, by freedom, you mean the freedom to purchase whatever you want, the freedom to go where—to have the resources to do whatever you want, if that's what you mean by freedom, then actually, automatically, whoever has more resources is more free.

Senator SANDERS. No. But my question was——

Mr. CANNON. When I——

Senator SANDERS. I'll give you a chance to respond. Please let me ask the question.

Mr. CANNON. Well, I think I am answering the question.

Senator SANDERS. My question is, you're not suggesting that the people of Denmark, and Finland, and Sweden are not free, by the conventional definition of the word?

Mr. CANNON. Economically, I believe they are less free. The conventional definition of the word is, do you have the freedom to do what you want with your life without being subject to physical restraint by others? And that could be the State. That could be other individuals, other than the State.

Senator SANDERS. And you think that is the condition in Scandinavia?

Mr. CANNON. Well, let me ask you this. If you had to pay——

Senator SANDERS. I'm asking you the questions.

Mr. CANNON. Well, but I'm a good Irishman, I'm going to answer a question with a question. If the government charged you a 100 percent tax rate, would you be free, if the government then provided you all of the material needs that an individual would want?

Senator SANDERS. I am not aware their governments or this government is charging people——

Mr. CANNON. Well—but to answer your question——

Senator SANDERS. I'll—excuse me.

Mr. CANNON [continuing]. I'm asking you——

Senator SANDERS. You can ask the questions when you get elected and I'll be over there, but at this moment, I'm asking the questions, OK? I think that's a hypothetical that is not terribly sensible.

Mr. CANNON. Well, then let——

Senator SANDERS. This is——

Mr. CANNON. Well, no.

Senator SANDERS This is——

Mr. CANNON. I think it is.

Senator SANDERS. OK, OK.

Mr. CANNON. I think it illustrates——

Senator SANDERS. Mr. Cannon, excuse me, please. Ms. Zolotorow, would you like to answer the question?

Mr. CANNON. I would appreciate the opportunity to answer your question.

Senator SANDERS. All right. You've had a considerable amount of time. I'll get back to you. But Ms. Zolotorow, would you like to answer the question?

Ms. ZOLOTOROW. Well, I think, if you're talking about freedom, when it comes to healthcare, if you are uninsured, you are not—you don't feel free to just get access to care. It is a job in itself. And you are penalized when you are sick and you are uninsured.

When you go to the emergency room, if you are admitted into the hospital, if you are insured, the hospital receives no compensation for the time you spent there, the emergency room, because they're an outpatient facility and the coding guideline is, if you are admitted from an outpatient facility, they forfeit their payment and the hospital gets paid, because the care you got there is considered the first initial hospital day.

But if you are uninsured, I get the bill for that. So I not only get the hospital bill from when I was admitted through the emergency room to the hospital. I got the bill for the emergency room, that an insured patient will not get. I get the hospital bill. I get all the doctors' bills. And I feel that that's a detriment to my freedom.

Senator SANDERS. OK. Thank you. Senator Merkley, you want to say something?

Senator MERKLEY. Thank you, Mr. Chair, and I think this is an important conversation. It takes me to my town halls. I have 36 town halls, one in each county each year, and I am one short of completing that for my third year.

I can't tell you how many times people come up to me and say, here's where I'm at: I'm in my late 50s, early 60s. I'm just trying to figure out how to bridge the gap until I can be under Medicare because my health problems and my inability to pay for them—basically dominate my life.

And we know, from many studies, that people delay, if you will, addressing their problems because they can't afford to. And then Medicare picks up the problems when they're more advanced and more troubling.

If we think of this in terms of quality of life, there's an awful lot of folks out there who feel like they could pursue what they'd like to pursue in life better if they didn't have the millstone of the costs of an extraordinarily expensive healthcare system around their neck.

And so I think there is kind of a double-edged sword here. We're arguing two sides of that issue. And I think it's a good discussion. I do want to end on the note, though, that the common ground that I feel is the point that Mr. Cannon made. We should be smart in studying what works. Oregon has been a leader in this. They've had some very controversial discussions about ranking, what procedures work the best, are most cost-effective, so that at any given level, you can afford to invest in insurance. You get the maximum public health effect from that.

That's a hard conversation for folks to have. People like to polarize the debate, but the fact is, every insurance policy has limits on what you cover and being smart about cost-effectiveness is an area that merits a lot of exploration. And I thank you all for your testimony on what is really such an important conversation to the quality of life in America.

Senator SANDERS. OK. Let me thank the panelists. And Mr. Cannon, maybe we will continue our discussion on the nature of human freedom at some other point. But thank you all very much for coming. Thank you.

[Whereupon, at 11:52 a.m., the hearing was adjourned.]

www.ingramcontent.com/pod-product-compliance
Lightning Source LLC
Chambersburg PA
CBHW052014280526
45793CB00005B/972